ETHNIC ELDERS' BENEFITS HANDBOOK

Sue Ward

BOOKS

Bulk orders

Age Concern England is pleased to offer customised editions of all its titles to UK companies, institutions or other organisations wishing to make a bulk purchase. For further information, please contact the Publishing Department at the address on this page. Tel: 0181-679 8000. Fax: 0181-679 6069. E-mail: addisom@ace.org.uk

Published by Age Concern England
1268 London Road
London SW16 4ER

First published 1997

Editor Gillian Clarke
Design and typesetting GreenGate Publishing Services, Tonbridge, Kent
Production Vinnette Marshall
Printed and bound in Great Britain by Bell & Bain Ltd, Glasgow

A catalogue record for this book is available from the British Library.
ISBN 0–86242–229–9

Contents

Foreword   vi

About the author   vii

Acknowledgements   viii

1 **Introduction**   I

Who this book is for   1
How to use this book   2
Where to look for further help   3

2 **Nationality law for older people**   5

The British Empire and the Commonwealth   5
British nationals who are not British citizens   11
People from the rest of the world   13
People born overseas of British fathers   13
How people become British   14

3 **Immigration law as it affects older people**   I7

EU citizens and their rights   19
Irish nationals   20
People who come under full immigration controls   20
Dependent relatives arriving to settle   23
Visiting the UK   27
Illegal entrants and overstayers   29
Repatriation   30
Refugees and asylum seekers   31
Appealing against immigration decisions   33

4 **Returning residents and immigration controls 37**

5 Social Security and people from other countries   39

What counts as the UK?   39
How Social Security is administered   40
Making a claim   41
If you feel a decision is wrong   43
People who are not fluent in English   45
Confusion over names   47
Links between the DSS and the Home Office   47
Use of Immigration Service records   48
Reciprocal agreements   48
EEA countries   49

6 National Insurance contributory benefits   51

State basic retirement pensions   51
Other pensions   59
Incapacity Benefit   60

7 Non-contributory benefits for people with disabilities   63

Severe Disablement Allowance   63
Disability Living Allowance   66
Attendance Allowance   67
Invalid Care Allowance   67

8 Income-related (means-tested) benefits   69

Income Support   69
Housing Benefit and Council Tax Benefit   81

9 The Social Fund   83

Community care grants   83
Crisis loans   84
Funeral costs   84

10 Health and social care   87

Primary health care   87
Hospital charges   87
Health costs abroad   89

Coming to the UK for private medical treatment 90
Community care and Social Services help 91

11 War pensions **94**

Claiming from abroad or going abroad 95

Appendix 1 Abbreviations and glossary **96**

**Appendix 2 Categories of countries for
immigration and Social Security purposes** **102**

Commonwealth countries 102
European Economic Area states 103
Countries from which entrants require a visa 103
Countries with which there is a reciprocal Social
Security agreement 105

**Appendix 3 Ethnic minority older
people in Britain** **107**

Appendix 4 Useful publications **109**

Appendix 5 Relevant DSS leaflets **111**

Appendix 6 Useful addresses **117**

About Age Concern **120**

Publications from Age Concern Books **121**

Index **124**

Foreword

Age Concern England is committed to fighting the cause of all older people in this country, irrespective of their cultural, religious and ethnic status. For some time now we have been working in partnership with the Commission for Racial Equality (CRE) to highlight the needs and issues affecting the increasing number of older people from ethnic minority groups and to provoke a response from policy makers and planners.

As part of this overall strategy, we are pleased to publish Sue Ward's *Ethnic Elders' Benefits Handbook* – an essential guide explaining key aspects of immigration and nationality law, and the range of benefits that are currently available depending upon individual circumstances. I warmly commend the book to you, and hope you find it of great benefit!

Sally Greengross
Director General
Age Concern England

About the author

Sue Ward is a freelance journalist and author specialising in pensions and Social Security matters. She is the author of Age Concern's annual *Pensions Handbook*, and also of *Changing Direction: Employment options in mid life*, published by Age Concern Books in 1996, as well as a number of other books and publications.

Sue is a member of her local Child Poverty Action Group branch and used to sit also on their national Executive Council. She does training for a number of unions and other bodies on pensions and Social Security matters, and has recently worked with the National Association of Citizens Advice Bureaux on a report on Incapacity Benefit. She sits on the local Social Security Appeals Tribunal in Newcastle upon Tyne, where the complexities of some of the cases on 'overseas benefits' sparked off her interest in this particular topic.

Acknowledgements

My thanks for their help go to Erif Rison and Alison Key of the National Association of Citizens Advice Bureaux (NACAB), Vivien Hughes and Jonathan Parr of the British Refugee Council, Brenda Thompson and her colleagues at the Benefits Agency's Pensions and Overseas Benefits Directorate, Duncan Lane of the London Advisory Service Alliance, and the Immigration Policy Directorate of the Home Office. Special thanks go to Sally West, the author of Age Concern's annual publication *Your Rights*, Sue Shutter as author of the Joint Council for the Welfare of Immigrants' (JCWI) *Immigration and Nationality Law Handbook*, and to all the authors of the Child Poverty Action Group's (CPAG) *Migration and Social Security Handbook*, on whose work I have drawn very heavily. I am very grateful to CPAG for letting me see their book at proof stage, and allowing me to make use of it. The opinions expressed here are my own and I take full responsibility for any mistakes and errors.

1 Introduction

Who this book is for

'Around 3 per cent of the ethnic minority population in the UK is aged 65 or over. While the numbers are relatively small, the needs and aspirations of ethnic minority older people are no less valid than those of the "majority" population. Taking the percentage at face value masks the huge increase in the numbers of ethnic minority older people over the coming two decades. It also "hides" the great diversity in culture, age discrimination and need for services between different ethnic minority populations.'

Source: *Age and Race; Double Discrimination,* Age Concern 1995

Age Concern is committed to working with the Commission for Racial Equality on a strategy aimed at improving the quality of life of older people from the ethnic minorities (ethnic elders). For some older people from non-white communities, an important area is income: research shows that the non-white population is at much greater risk of poverty than the white population. Non-white pensioner households are much less likely to be receiving retirement pension or occupational pensions, and more likely to rely on Income Support and Housing Benefit, than are white pensioner households.

Our Social Security system contains many 'barriers to benefit' for ethnic elders. Some of these are structural, as the system is largely based on contributions made by people over a working lifetime in this country; some are legal, with special restrictions on 'persons from abroad' claiming certain benefits. Others include language barriers and low take-up owing to ignorance of one's rights or fear of stigma. A recent study has found that how people regard benefits is strongly influenced by cultural and religious factors. Negative views and a sense of shame when claiming were strong, particularly among Bangladeshi, Pakistani and Chinese households and communities.

This book is intended to help any older person from an ethnic minority, and those seeking to advise them, to understand how the system works, what their rights are and how they can claim a Social Security benefit to which they are entitled.

For many older members of ethnic minority groups, the rights to Social Security benefits will be no different from those of anyone else, if they have full UK citizenship or have spent all their working lives in the UK. But for many others, and indeed for many people who were born in the UK but have spent much or all of their working lives abroad, there are special rules to cope with in an already complex system.

There are probably also many thousands of younger people who would like older relatives who are currently abroad to come to live with them, if they could find a way to bring them over and to support them. And there must be at least as many older people who are currently in the UK but would like to go abroad, either to their place of birth or some other country, if they were able to do this without losing their income.

It is all these people and their advisers that this book is designed to help. It can be difficult to find general information that is relevant, if you don't know the detailed questions you need to ask. Specialist agencies and support groups for particular communities have built up considerable expertise. But much of what is available, and many of the legal cases, concentrate on people of working age and on the rights of those who are citizens of the European Union (EU), rather than on those of older people from elsewhere. So this book aims to fill the gap.

How to use this book

This book is intended to help ordinary people through the maze of law on immigration and citizenship, and on related Social Security rights for those at or near pension age. It is written to be understood by people who are not experts, and who have problems or questions to which they are trying to find a solution. The rules about nationality and immigration use many special terms, which will be unfamiliar to anyone who is not an expert. To help readers, these terms are explained in the Glossary (pp 97–101).

I have assumed that readers will be mostly people in their late 50s and beyond, or their friends, relatives or advisers trying to help with their problems. I'm also assuming that people will already have finished their working lives and retired, or are close to doing so and are planning for the future beyond work. So this book summarises immigration and citizenship law as it is likely to affect older people but does *not* cover, for instance, work permits. On Social Security benefits, it deals with pensions, widows' benefits, benefits for those who are sick or disabled, and the means-tested benefits such as Income Support, but *not* Jobseeker's Allowance or Child Benefit.

Including full details of all the Social Security benefits covered would have made this book very long. It would also have duplicated other Age Concern publications that are easily available and are updated each year, especially *Your Rights*. So I have given only very a brief summary of the benefits themselves, assuming that readers will be able to refer to *Your Rights* for fuller information. I have also given references for the relevant leaflets from the Department of Social Security (DSS); the ones that refer specifically to benefits for people coming from or going to other countries are listed on pages 111–116.

Where to look for further help

For immigration and nationality law, the main book is the *Immigration and Nationality Law Handbook*, published by the Joint Council for the Welfare of Immigrants. On benefits issues, the most detailed guide is the *Migration and Social Security Handbook: A rights guide for people entering and leaving the UK*, published by Child Poverty Action Group (see 'Useful publications', p 109). Both these books are comprehensive, and excellent for advisers, but rather detailed for ordinary people to find their way through.

To get individual advice independent of the official bodies, try the local Citizens Advice Bureau, or the local Law Centre if there is one. For immigration and nationality issues, they may need to refer you on, but are likely to know which local solicitors specialise in the subject, and also whether there is a suitable support group in your area. The major national body dealing with these issues is the Joint Council for the Welfare of Immigrants (JCWI) (see 'Useful addresses', p 118). For people who have been or are trying to obtain refugee status, there is the Refugee Council.

In each local area there is also a Racial Equality Council (REC). The aims of RECs are to eliminate racial discrimination and to provide equality of opportunity between different racial and ethnic groups. They should also be able to tell you about associations, support groups and specialist services (such as interpreting) for particular ethnic groups. You can find the address of your local REC in the phone directory or through your local library's information services.

Many local authorities have Welfare Rights Officers who specialise in Social Security benefit issues. A few have specialists working with particular communities, such as the Chinese. At national level, the Citizens' Rights Office of Child Poverty Action Group can give advice on particularly knotty problems (see 'Useful addresses').

For help with more general problems relating to older people, contact your local Age Concern group, or the national Age Concern organisations. Age Concern England publishes a whole range of books, some of which are listed on pp 121–122. There are also factsheets, which go into more detail on many topics.

If someone seems to be running into particular problems or is suffering hardship because of the way the rules work, it may be worth contacting the local MP (even for someone who is not eligible to vote). He or she will be able to take up a case with the Home Office or the Department of Social Security. Staff at your local reference library should be able to tell you who is the MP for a particular area. If the problem arises because of rules or bureaucratic delays in another country, you could ask their Embassy or High Commission for details of the equivalent representatives there.

2 Nationality law for older people

Many of the people for whom this book is intended will have come to the UK many years ago, when the laws on both nationality and immigration were quite different. This chapter gives a broad summary of the law on nationality in the UK. It is intended mainly to set the scene, and to explain some of the terms that will be used frequently in the book. For more detail, look in the *Immigration and Nationality Law Handbook* (details on p 109).

Immigration and nationality are two different areas of law. **Nationality** simply defines the country of which you are a citizen, and which usually issues you with a passport. **Immigration** law is the system of rules by which each country decides who may live in that country and under what conditions. This chapter outlines the nationality issues, and Chapter 3 the immigration ones.

The British Empire and the Commonwealth

The British Empire, 'on which the sun never sets', existed until well after World War II as a mixture of colonies, dependencies and protectorates. A large proportion of the immigration into the UK since World War II has been from these countries. Most (apart from the Falkland Islands, Gibraltar and a scattering of tiny islands) are now independent but remain members of the Commonwealth.

Nationality (and immigration) rights for people from these countries have always been different from those for people in other parts of the world. But they have changed substantially over the last 50 years, and the position of older people today will depend on such factors as:

• date of birth;

- when they arrived in the UK;
- what the status of their country of origin was then (and perhaps also what it is now).

So the next few sections look at the historical position, what has changed over the years, and how this affects the position of people currently in the UK or seeking to come here.

Before 1949

Until 1949, anyone born in, or with a connection with, the UK or a British colony or dependency was a British subject.

There was also a small group of British protected persons, born in or connected with a protectorate such as one of the Indian princely states or Northern Nigeria. They are treated in international law as British nationals, but in UK law they are treated as aliens.

Between 1949 and 1962

In 1949 the British Nationality Act 1948 created the status of citizen of the United Kingdom and Colonies (CUKC) for people born in, or with a connection with, the UK and its remaining colonies. The Act recognised the existence of independent Commonwealth countries with their own citizenship, and also retained the status of British subject. This was held by all citizens of the UK and colonies, and all other Commonwealth citizens – virtually a dual citizenship. All British subjects had the same rights, principally the 'right of abode' in the UK (explained on p 100) without having to meet any immigration requirements. British protected persons remained in the same position as before 1949. There were also British subjects without citizenship, mainly people from India and Pakistan who had failed to acquire the citizenship of their newly independent countries but who were not eligible for CUKC status.

As the different countries became independent, the normal process was for people in those countries to lose their CUKC status, provided that they gained citizenship of their country, but to retain their status as British subjects. They were then classified as both Commonwealth citizens and British subjects, and so had full rights of entry and abode in the UK. People with CUKC status were therefore a group of those born in or connected with the UK or its remaining colonies, within a much larger group of British subjects.

Between 1962 and 1983

During this period, the immigration rights of various categories of British subjects became more restricted, their right of abode (also called 'patriality' between 1973 and 1983) being withdrawn in some cases.

CUKCs who had acquired their citizenship in the UK (through birth, registration or naturalisation), who had a parent or grandparent who had acquired CUKC status in the UK, or who had themselves lived in the UK for five years or more and become settled here, kept their right of abode. Others, for instance East African Asians, lost it. Commonwealth citizens who had a parent born in the UK, or were women married to a man with right of abode, were also able to retain or gain it. CUKC passports were endorsed on page 5 if the holder had right of abode.

British Nationality Act 1981

This came into effect on 1 January 1983. It abolished CUKC status and changed the way people can acquire British nationality. It created three new types of citizenship:

- British citizenship for people who, at 31 December 1982, were CUKCs with right of abode in the UK.
- British Dependent Territories citizenship for people who were CUKCs because of a connection with a country that was still a British dependency (such as Hong Kong).
- British Overseas citizenship for other CUKCs without right of abode or a connection with a British dependency (such as East African Asians).

Since then, Falkland Islanders have been made into full British citizens, while Hong Kong people who were British Dependent Territories citizens have been given the opportunity to acquire a different status, that of British National (Overseas) but without any right of abode in the UK. British protected persons have remained in the same position as before. People who had been classed as 'British subjects without citizenship' (see p 6) were confusingly renamed 'British subjects' but, except for them, this status was abolished.

See the flowchart opposite for details of who has had right of entry and who has not.

What type of citizenship?

The passport will sometimes (but not always) give the exact status of the holder. Most British passports issued before 1 January 1983 describe the holder as 'British subject; citizen of the UK and Colonies' on page 1. Page 5 should say 'holder has the right of abode in the UK'. If this is in the passport and not cancelled, it is likely that the holder became a British citizen on 1 January 1983 without needing to do anything about it.

If the words on page 5 have been cancelled, the holder is likely to be a British Dependent Territories citizen or British Overseas citizen, without the right of abode. He or she will therefore be affected by the immigration laws explained in the next chapter. British protected persons and British subjects do not have a right of abode either (except a small group, mainly married women).

It is always worth checking where people do not have right of abode, in case there has been an error. Also check that nothing has happened to change the person's status since the passport was issued – for instance, has that country become independent since that date? There are also some special groups:

- People from the Caribbean countries that gained their independence in 1981 or later took citizenship of the new country. If they had lived in the UK for more than five years and were settled before independence, they kept their British citizenship. This applies to people from Belize, St Kitts-Nevis, and Antigua and Barbuda.
- Some people, including many from Hong Kong, have British travel documents (brown documents called a certificate of identity) but are not any kind of British nationals – in effect they are stateless and have no special rights.

Passports issued on or after 1 January 1983 describe people's nationality status on the same page as their personal details.

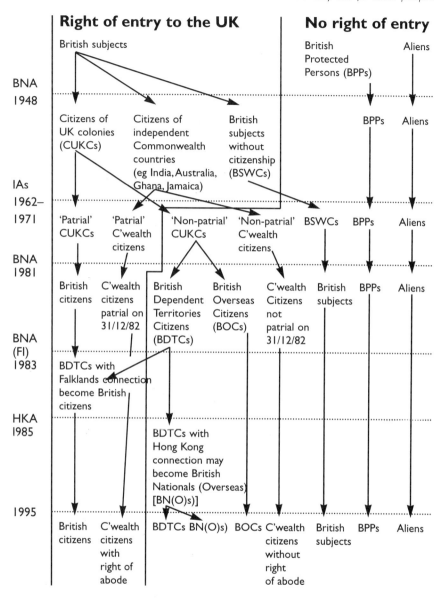

The development of immigration and nationality law
Source: *Immigration and Nationality Handbook*
BNA = *British Nationality Act*   HKA = *Hong Kong Act*
FI   = *Falkland Islands*   IA   = *Immigration Act*

British citizen passports issued on or after 1 January 1983 do not have an endorsement stating that they have right of abode, as this is automatic. People may be worried that this means their right of abode has been withdrawn, but can be reassured that this is not the case.

No other British nationals have a right of abode in the UK, except a few British subjects. They should have an endorsement in their passport called 'certificates of entitlement to the right of abode' (explained on p 100).

See the flowchart below for details of who is a British citizen. The chart covers *only* people born before 1 January 1983; the rules are different for anyone born later.

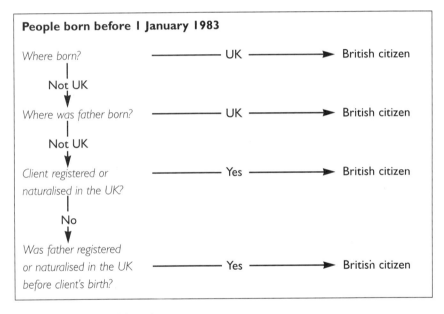

Who is a British citizen?
Source: *Immigration and Nationality Law Handbook*

An important point is that 'parent' or 'father' applies to men only if they were legally married. If they married after the child's birth, it depends on the law of the country where the marriage took place whether it automatically legitimates the child, or whether any special procedures have to be followed.

British nationals who are not British citizens

As explained above, in general British **nationals** who are not British **citizens** do not have the right of abode. So British status is only really a travel document facility, and does not give them the right to live anywhere. However, British Overseas citizens who have been admitted for settlement in the UK *do* have a right to be readmitted for settlement at any time. They can ask the Home Office to endorse their passport to say this. This means that, even if they stay away from the UK for more than two years at a time, they cannot be refused 'indefinite leave to remain' – that is, permission to stay without a time limit or other restriction on when they return.

British nationals with an East African connection

In the late 1960s, British nationals living in East and Central Africa, most of whose families came from the Indian sub-continent, came under pressure to leave some of the newly independent countries, especially Uganda and Kenya. This led to the passing of the Commonwealth Immigrants Act of 1968, restricting their right of entry to the UK. But at the same time, the Government announced the creation of a special 'quota voucher' scheme to admit a small number of these British nationals who were being pressed to leave the countries they were in. In 1972 there was a large scale expulsion of British nationals of Asian origin from Uganda, many of whom had to go to India to wait for vouchers under this scheme if they wanted to enter the UK.

There is still a queue of people applying for these vouchers, though waiting time in India (having been very long in the past) is now down to three months after an application is made. Around 500 vouchers a year are being issued. Only heads of households (which means men) can qualify, but families can be admitted to accompany or join them in the UK. The voucher-holder does not have to fulfil the 'public funds' rule (explained on p 26), but their families do, and support and accommodation must be provided by the voucher-holder.

Once admitted, a voucher-holder is allowed to remain for an indefinite period (that is, for settlement). Their families are admitted for a year initially and may then qualify for settlement.

British nationals from Hong Kong

Most British nationals in Hong Kong lost the right to live in the UK under the Commonwealth Immigrants Act 1962. But those who were

- born, registered or naturalised in the UK, or
- had parents or grandparents who were, or
- had spent five years continuously in the UK before 1983 and became settled here (or women married to men who met these conditions)

could retain their right of abode; they became both British citizens *and*, until 30 June 1997, British Dependent Territories citizens. The rest were solely British Dependent Territories citizens (BDTCs), and were allowed to apply for the status of British National (Overseas) before 1 July 1997, but this gives them no right to travel to the UK.

If they did not apply, they may have lost British nationality altogether when Hong Kong returned to China. People of Chinese ethnic origin are understood to be Chinese citizens; the rest (eg people of Indian origin who have lived in Hong Kong for many years) automatically became British Overseas Citizens if they would otherwise have been stateless. The British Nationality (Hong Kong) Act 1997, which came into force on 19 March 1997, enables people from non-Chinese ethnic minorities in Hong Kong who are *solely* British nationals to apply for registration as British citizens. To be entitled to registration, applicants must be ordinarily resident in Hong Kong, which is where applications must normally be made. However, applications from people in the UK who think they are eligible for registration can be made to the Home Office Nationality Directorate in Liverpool. Because of the anxiety about what might happen after the Chinese take-over in 1997, the Government agreed in 1989 to register up to 50,000 key workers in Hong Kong (mostly BDTCs) as British citizens.

People from Hong Kong living in the UK can fall into several categories. Anyone with a brown Certificate of Identity is not a British national at all; he or she was born in mainland China and is probably entitled to Chinese citizenship (but could become naturalised British, see p 99).

Someone with a British passport should have right of abode if:

- the passport states on page 5 that the holder has right of abode in the UK, or describes the person as a British citizen (as explained in the sections above);

- the person has lived legally in the UK for at least five years before 1 January 1983, without conditions on their stay at the end of the period;
- the person was born in the UK before 1983.

If none of these applies, look at the passport stamp to see what the immigration status is, as explained in the next chapter.

People from the rest of the world

Since the early part of the twentieth century, anyone who was not a British subject was classified as an alien, and their right of entry to the UK was restricted by various Aliens Acts. These applied, for instance, to people fleeing from Nazi persecution before World War II, or to stateless people or ex-prisoners of war settling in the UK after that war.

Little changed for 'aliens' after 1949, until Britain joined the European Economic Community, with its expansion and the gradual evolution of the rules on 'rights of free movement' which have brought new rights for citizens of those countries. These rights also apply to people who left their country before it joined the Community (or even before this existed), so long as they have kept their original citizenship, as well as to more recent emigrants.

> **Stephanos** came to the UK in 1968, well before his country of origin Greece joined the European Community. But he has retained his citizenship, and so will still be treated in the same way as his Greek neighbour who has come in the last few years.

Immigration rights for EU citizens, and those in the wider European Economic Area (EEA), are considered in Chapter 3.

People born overseas of British fathers

People born before 1 January 1983 with a British father (not mother) automatically became British citizens if their father acquired his citizenship in the UK either:

- by being born or adopted by a UK citizen father, in the UK; or
- by being registered or naturalised in the UK before the child was born.

In some cases, having a British grandfather but not father can confer British nationality – see the *Immigration and Nationality Law Handbook* for details.

People born overseas who acquire British citizenship because one or both of their parents is a British citizen are classified as British citizens by descent, and cannot automatically pass on citizenship to *their* children born overseas.

There are some special rules for the children born abroad of such groups as diplomats, people working for the British Council overseas, and members of the armed forces. Look in the *Immigration and Nationality Law Handbook* for details.

How people become British

People who come into the UK to settle have the option to retain their previous citizenship or to become **naturalised** or (for a few adults) **registered**.

Naturalisation

Before you apply for naturalisation, you must be settled – that is, there must be no time limit on your stay in the UK under the immigration laws, which in most cases will mean you have been granted indefinite leave to enter or remain in the UK. Your application will lead to your immigration status being investigated, so anyone whose status is irregular in any way (or has been in the past) needs to take advice before applying. It is not cheap to apply for British citizenship, and the Home Office keeps the fee even if the application fails, so there is no point in wasting the money unnecessarily. However, the decision to grant naturalisation rests completely with the Home Office, and there is no right of appeal if you are turned down.

You apply by filling in form AN, available from the Home Office Nationality Directorate, and sending the fee at the same time. The applications can take a very long time to process – about 9 months in summer 1996. The basic requirements are:

- you are resident and settled in the UK;
- you have sufficient knowledge of the language;

- you are of good character;
- you intend to live in the UK.

People married to British citizens do not need to satisfy the 'language' or 'intention' requirements.

Taking these in turn, people who are not married to British citizens must have been living legally in the UK for five years continuously, and must have been physically present in the UK on the date five years before they apply. They must not have been absent for more than 450 days in that time, and they should have been settled for at least a year before they apply.

The conditions for people who are married to British citizens are slightly easier: they must have been living in the UK for three years, and have been physically present in the UK on the date three years before they apply. They must be settled at the time they apply.

On language, people who are not married to British citizens must show that they have 'sufficient knowledge' of English, Welsh or Scottish Gaelic. This means that they should be able to converse in it, though they need not be able to read and write in the language. This is assessed by the Nationality Directorate or sometimes the police – usually by a visit or interview, occasionally by a telephone call. Sometimes a police interview is conducted for other reasons, for instance to assess whether the 'good character' requirement has been met. It can be a shock to people to have a police officer turn up at their house, and there has been criticism of the way the interviews are conducted.

The test of 'good character' is very poorly defined. Criminal convictions, including motoring offences, are taken into account, and checks are also usually made on financial status and any security risk.

On the intention to live in the UK, if someone wants to travel abroad while their application is pending, they will need to show that their absence is temporary (for example, in order to study abroad).

Registration

British nationals who are not British citizens (see p 98 for an explanation of this) can gain citizenship by registration rather than by naturalisation. The residence and settlement requirements are broadly the same as those for naturalisation for someone not married to a British citizen, and if you qualify you cannot be refused. But this right is more theoretical than real, because it is very difficult for most people in these categories to gain settlement rights in the UK unless they qualify for special quota vouchers (as explained on p 11), as they are subject to immigration controls. Immigration law is explained in the next chapter.

3 Immigration law as it affects older people

This chapter gives a broad summary of the law on immigration to the UK. It is intended mainly to set the scene, and to explain some of the terms that are used. For more detail, look in the *Immigration and Nationality Law Handbook* (details on p 109).

As explained in the last chapter, immigration and nationality are two different areas of law. **Immigration** law is the system of rules by which each country decides who is able to live in that country and under what conditions. In Britain, not everybody who has British nationality is automatically able to enter the UK as a citizen, as explained below.

British citizens, and citizens of other Commonwealth countries (see Appendix 2 for a list of Commonwealth countries) with 'right of abode', are free to come into and go from the UK, and to live in the UK, and do not need permission to enter. But they may need to prove what their status is, and they may find that they are questioned by immigration officials at their port of entry.

It should be clear from your passport whether you have right of abode or not. A British citizen will generally have a British passport with 'British citizen' stated on page 1 of the old style passports, and on the back page of the new style passports. If you are a Commonwealth citizen with right of abode, there should be a 'certificate of patriality' in a passport issued before 1 January 1983 or a 'certificate of entitlement' in one issued after that date. If not, or if you are not travelling on a British passport, it is possible to get a certificate of entitlement as proof of status, in the form of a sticker in your passport. This is obtained from the British Embassy or High Commission, before travelling, or from the Home Office in the UK. People who arrive in the UK claiming to have right of abode but without the right passport or certificate are likely to find themselves returned to the country they have travelled from. They have a right of appeal, but will have to exercise it from that other country.

Right of abode is a special status, available only to Commonwealth citizens born before 1 January 1983 who had a parent born in the UK, and to women who were Commonwealth citizens on 31 December 1982, and were married before 1 January 1983 to a man who was a British citizen or had the right of abode in the UK.

Citizens of Ireland are in a special category, because the UK and Ireland, together with the Isle of Man and the Channel Islands, form a Common Travel Area (CTA). So British citizens travelling to Ireland automatically have right of residence in Ireland, and Irish people can live in the UK without being subject to immigration controls.

Citizens of other countries in the European Economic Area have certain rights, explained later in this chapter. People from all other countries are subject to immigration controls, and may need visas before they come to the UK even for a short time, as explained below. They may also come up against immigration controls when they enter the UK, if they re-enter the UK after an absence.

Ravi has an Indian passport but has lived in the UK for many years. He goes to India to see his family when he retires from his job. He falls ill during the visit and the return half of his airline ticket expires. Before they will sell him a new one, the airline insists that he must provide them with full details of his immigration status and family and housing in the UK, because they are afraid he may not be eligible for entry to the UK and they could be fined for having an inadequately documented passenger.

The Home Office and Immigration Service stamp passports to show people's immigration status. For this reason, if you are travelling for the first time on a new passport, it is sensible to carry the old passport as well, so that the Immigration Officer can immediately see what your status is. Then the appropriate stamp is usually given again, so that your status will be clear to other Immigration Officers in the future. It's then no longer necessary to carry the old passport as well as the new when travelling, but it should be kept somewhere safe, in case the evidence is ever required.

EU citizens and their rights

The European Union (EU) has 15 member states, which are listed on page 103. In addition, there are three states with special treaties with the EU – Iceland, Liechtenstein and Norway – and together they make up the European Economic Area (EEA). Nationals of these 18 countries have the right to freedom of movement within the EEA. But people of other nationalities living in EU countries do not have rights of entry or rights of residence in other EU countries. There are special rights for some nationals of other countries with Association Agreements with the EEA, such as Turkey and some eastern European countries.

Workers (including self-employed people) have the right to take up jobs in other EU states, and to remain in the state in which they have been working when they retire. They also have the right to bring in members of their family. 'Family' for this purpose means spouse and children, and also dependent parents and grandparents. There is also a general obligation on a member state to consider sympathetically the admission of other family members, if they are dependent on the worker or were living under his or her roof in the country from which they came.

> **Rosa** is aged 70, and has lived with her niece Ella and Ella's husband in Italy for several years. When Ella gets a job in Bristol, she is able to bring both her husband and Rosa to live with her here.

The right of residence was extended to pensioners by a 1992 change in the law: they may settle in another member state, even if they have never previously been there. If you want to do this:

- you must have been employed or self-employed in your own member state, or be part of the family of someone who was;
- you must be receiving an invalidity or early retirement pension, or old age benefit or another pension that will enable you to live independently ('sufficient to avoid becoming a burden on the Social Security system of the host member state'); and
- you must be covered by sickness insurance in respect of all risks in the host member state.

This right is being used quite heavily now by British citizens wanting to retire to Spain or France; but it can equally be used by, for instance, Spanish or French pensioners who think that Blackpool or Bournemouth is just the thing for a bracing retirement! However, the 'habitual residence' rules (covered in detail in Chapter 8) could prevent them claiming UK Income Support if it turned out that they did not have enough to live on.

You should apply for a residence permit if you are making use of your European immigration rights. You do this by obtaining application form EEC1 from a JobCentre or from the Home Office, and sending it to the Home Office with the required photos and your passport. If a permit is issued, it is normally for five years; after four years holding a residence permit, an EEA national may apply for settlement.

Family members who want to come with someone using their EU treaty rights need an 'EEA family permit' (and also a visa if they are themselves 'visa nationals', see p 101). The permit is issued free, and the British Embassy or High Commission or the Home Office will grant it for the same length of time as for the EEA national's residence permit.

As a result of an important judgment in the European Court in 1992, the Surinder Singh case, it is possible to exercise these free movement rights to return to your *own* state. It may be possible to use the same case law to bring in non-EEA elderly relatives without the strict 'public funds' rules (explained on p 26) that would otherwise be applied.

Irish nationals

Ireland is a member of the EEA, so their nationals come under the rules explained above. There is no immigration control between the UK and the Republic of Ireland, which is part of the Common Travel Area along with the Isle of Man and the Channel Islands. So Irish and British citizens are exempt from immigration control when they travel between the two countries.

People who come under full immigration controls

People who are not in one of the groups explained above will find that they are subject to full immigration controls, and will need to get 'leave' (permission) to enter the UK. This is granted when someone actually arrives at the point of entry to the UK. In addition, most people (ie 'visa nationals' – see below) have to obtain **entry clearance** before travelling to the UK. They must do this in the country from which they are leaving. Getting past this hurdle does not give them a right to enter the UK, but simply demonstrates that they are eligible to do so. So people who have gone through all the right formalities can still be turned away when they reach the UK, as explained below.

There is a long list of countries (see Appendix 2) whose citizens are defined as **visa nationals** – that is, they need a visa (entry clearance) before they can come to the UK. Stateless persons also need visas. Visa nationals need to arrive with passports (or other travel documents) endorsed with a UK visa for the purpose for which they seek entry, even if their visit is planned to be temporary. They get this from the UK High Commission, Embassy or Consulate before travelling. Without a visa, it's unlikely that a visa national will find an airline or shipping company willing to carry them to the UK, as it could be fined £2000 for doing so.

Non-visa nationals (that is, people from any other country not listed in Appendix 2) also require entry clearance if they are coming for certain purposes, such as a dependant coming for settlement. In effect, almost every older person coming to the UK to be with their relatives, apart from those with the right sort of British/Commonwealth or EEA passport (as explained in Chapter 2), will need entry clearance.

Retired people of independent means

Since October 1994, people who are at least 60 years old, and with a guaranteed income of at least £25,000 a year without working, doing business or getting help from anyone else, or claiming public funds, may be allowed to come and live in the UK. They must apply for entry clearance and show that they have enough money and that they plan to live on it. They also have to intend to make their main home the UK and show that they have a 'close connection' with the UK. Their spouses (and children under 18) can also apply for entry clearance under this rule.

People in this group will normally be given permission to stay for four years on arrival, but they are not allowed to work. Near the end of the four years they can apply to settle. This will be granted so long as the money on which they are relying has remained available throughout the period, they have made the UK their main home, and they have not needed to have 'recourse to public funds' (that is, they have not applied for certain state benefits or housing for homeless people; see the Glossary for details).

Getting leave to enter

Anyone who needs 'leave to enter' will be questioned by an Immigration Officer on their arrival. They will then be:

- given indefinite leave; or
- given limited leave; or
- refused leave to enter.

Or they may be asked to undergo a further examination, for instance if there are enquiries to be made. While waiting for this, they will either be detained or given temporary admission, possibly on bail. This may also happen if someone is claiming asylum as a refugee (see p 31).

A decision granting or refusing leave to enter must be given in writing no later than 24 hours after the Immigration Officer has completed his or her examination. If such a written decision is not given in this time, the individual is assumed to have been granted leave to enter the UK for six months, but is not allowed to take a job.

Someone who arrives in the UK with the proper entry clearance can still be refused entry, but only on certain grounds. The list below does not go into all of these, but only those likely to be relevant to older people.

- **False representation** – if a false statement was made in order to gain entry clearance. Individuals themselves might not know that this was done, if, for instance, they had employed an agent to sort out the paperwork and the agent had said something untrue, but entry could still be refused.
- **Not disclosing a material fact** – something that would have affected the decision to give entry clearance was not disclosed at the time of application. Again, the individual could be unaware that a material fact had not been disclosed, but entry could still be refused.
- **Change of circumstance** – if something important has changed since the clearance was given, this may remove the basis for admission. So, for instance, if someone was coming to join a relative in the

UK, but this relative died while they were on their way, entry could now be refused.

- **On medical grounds** – if someone intends to stay more than six months, or if the Medical Inspector advises that the person has a specified disease or condition, the Immigration Officer may refuse leave to enter, unless there are strong compassionate grounds.

There's a right of appeal against being refused entry. For someone who arrives without entry clearance, the appeal can only be made from outside the UK, and the person will have to leave immediately. Someone who has arrived *with* entry clearance can appeal from within the UK. It is important to get proper advice, as quickly as possible, because the deadlines can be very tight.

If the stamp in your passport is not clear

If the stamp in your passport is illegible or defective, you are deemed to have been given leave to enter for six months, with a condition preventing you from taking a job. However, if you entered before 10 July 1988 and had a defective or illegible stamp, you are deemed to have been given **indefinite** leave to enter.

Dependent relatives arriving to settle

Many UK residents will have family elsewhere, and may wish to bring them over so that the whole family can live together. In that case, the person already in the UK will need to act as 'sponsor' and deal with the complex arrangements at this end. The applicant has to apply from abroad, but the sponsor must be 'settled' in the UK (for an explanation of 'settled', see p 100). This section concentrates on what happens with older people – the law for children and people of working age is rather different.

In the countries of the Indian sub-continent, people over 70 years old applying for settlement are considered in a priority queue, so they should not have to wait long for an interview. There are no special provisions made for older people in other countries.

It's important to remember that if someone applies for settlement with their relatives and is turned down, this is likely to make it more difficult to obtain a visitor's visa in future.

People who arrive on a visit and then apply for permanent settlement still have to meet the rules explained below. There is a danger that they could be treated as illegal entrants, if the Home Office decides that it was always their plan to settle in the UK and they obtained entry under false pretences.

Parents and grandparents

Parents and grandparents over 65 can be given entry clearance to join their (adult) children and grandchildren in the UK, under certain conditions. The main ones are that:

- people who qualify are widowed mothers, grandmothers, fathers or grandfathers, or parents or grandparents arriving as a couple; the individual concerned must be over 65; or, for a couple, at least one of them must be over 65;
- they are wholly or mainly dependent on sons or daughters who are settled in the UK; this means that *before* coming to the UK they must have been financially dependent on their children in the UK;
- they are without close relatives to turn to in their own country or, if they do have such relatives, these relatives are unable to support them;
- there will be an adequate home for them, without 'recourse to public funds' (explained on p. 26), in accommodation that the sponsoring child owns or occupies;
- their sponsoring child is able and willing to maintain them adequately, without 'recourse to public funds'.

There are some extra rules where a parent has remarried: he or she must be unable to look to the spouse or children of the second marriage for support, *and* the children in the UK must have sufficient means and accommodation to maintain the spouse and any children as well, if they also arrive as dependants.

Some people will be exempt from these rules because of the different rules for citizens of the EEA. 'Relatives in the ascending line' – parents, grandparents, and great-grandparents – have the right to join an EEA citizen who has travelled to another EEA country to work there. They could also be the relatives of a non-EEA spouse of an EEA citizen.

> **Joan O'Connor** was born in Colombia, and is now married to an Irishman
> living and working in the UK. So she can make use of these rules if her
> elderly parents want to come to live with her

Some older parents or grandparents (or indeed other relatives) may have
'right of abode' in the UK, as explained on page 100, even if their children do not, and could again be exempt from the immigration controls.

Other relatives

Other relatives, such as uncles and aunts, or mothers who are not widowed, have to meet the conditions listed above (except for age), *and* be
living alone in the most exceptional circumstances. Very few people
manage to achieve entry under these rules.

What do the requirements mean?

Dependency This means mainly financial support, but other forms of
dependence are not excluded, such as emotional dependence. It could
make all the difference to a decision to admit or not, if someone was
being mainly rather than completely supported financially by their relative but had very strong emotional ties. From the various cases that
have come to court, 'dependence' seems to be interpreted as meaning
something stronger than the 'normal love and affection of a united
family'. Needing someone to turn to for support in cases of chronic illness or emergency might also carry some weight.

In any case, the dependence must be a matter of need rather than choice.
If you have sufficient income or assets to support yourself without help
from your children, you are not wholly or mainly dependent. If you have
other relatives who would be willing and able to meet the needs your
sponsor is providing, you will also not be counted as dependent.

> In one 1989 case, a widowed mother had only one son, with whom she had
> lived for 40 years. She applied for admission as his dependant. The court
> decided that her reliance on his society and support should be regarded as
> an emotional need which no other relative could provide.

Recourse to public funds For the purposes of the immigration rules, 'public funds' are Income Support, Family Credit, Housing Benefit, Council Tax Benefit, Attendance Allowance, Invalid Care Allowance, Severe Disablement Allowance, Disability Living Allowance, Disability Working Allowance and the means-tested element of the Jobseeker's Allowance, and housing provided by the local authority for homeless people. So before people get entry clearance, they have to show that they, or the sponsoring relatives, can support themselves without needing to apply for any of these benefits. The sponsor may have to give a written undertaking to be responsible for the person's maintenance and accommodation. (There is no objection to the sponsor claiming any of these benefits in their own right.)

In the past, the 'public funds' condition was not normally endorsed in a person's passport, and immigration officials did not necessarily tell someone that he or she (or a spouse or dependant) was subject to it. So people already in the UK may not be aware that it affects them, and it's advisable to check first with an adviser who understands the law. However, under the 1996 Asylum and Immigration Act, this can be made a formal condition and so included in the passport.

Note In addition to these 'public funds' rules, there are important new restrictions on people from abroad (including those who have been sponsored) claiming a number of Social Security benefits. These are covered in Chapter 8.

Accommodation There must be evidence that there will be adequate accommodation, owned or occupied by that person or their sponsor, available on their arrival in the UK. It must be fit in terms of the environmental or public health requirements, and not involve overcrowding. The ownership or tenancy must be legal and reasonably secure. The immigration rules say that the sponsor should own or occupy the accommodation exclusively – it must be for the exclusive use of the sponsor and his or her dependants. The unit of accommodation could be as small as a bedroom in a shared property, however.

Visiting the UK

Many people have relatives or friends who do not want to settle in the UK but would like to visit them. The Immigration Rules were changed in 1994 to create some special rules for people in transit or medical visitors (covered in Chapter 10). For any other sort of visit, people who are visa nationals (explained on p 101) need to obtain entry clearance from a British High Commission or Embassy before travelling. Those who are not visa nationals do not need entry clearance in advance, but may prefer to obtain it anyway. Although it gives some assurance that a person will be admitted, the refusal rate for those applying for entry clearance from overseas is higher than for those who apply when they arrive.

The rules on visitors are that people must:

- be genuinely seeking entry for not more than six months as a visitor;
- intend to leave at the end of their visit;
- not intend taking a job (or studying at a state school);
- maintain and accommodate themselves and any dependants with the resources available to them, or be maintained and accommodated by relatives or friends, without recourse to public funds (for details of what this set of conditions means, see p 26);
- be able to meet the costs of their outward and return journeys, either because they already have a return ticket or because they can show that they have the means to purchase one; and
- not be someone to whom any of the general reasons for refusing entry applies (covered in pp 22–23).

The most difficult of these conditions is the 'intention' test. People have to satisfy the immigration official that they genuinely intend leaving at the end of their visit, and the official then uses his or her judgement about whether to believe them. The official may ask detailed questions about a person's life and background to see if they believe the answers. They may ask, for instance, 'Will you need to go back after only two weeks? Who is looking after your house/farm while you are away? Can you afford to spend this amount of money in so short a time?' They may search luggage and read any correspondence, including letters carried by the person to give to other people in the UK.

If there are definite reasons that visitors have to return, it is wise to try to bring evidence of this – for example, commitments to other people or the fact that they have left someone temporarily in charge of a farm or house. But according to the *Immigration and Nationality Law Handbook* 'Immigration Officers will openly admit to using something they call "nose" – their alleged sixth sense telling them when someone is not genuine.'

To find out whether a person meets the 'support and accommodation' test, officers will ask for evidence of how much money they, or their friends and relatives, have, and where they are intending to stay. So people need evidence such as their bank statements, if they are bringing their own money. If they will be supported by their friends or relatives in the UK, people should obtain a letter of invitation from them confirming their willingness to support the visitor while in the UK, and copies of bank statements or other resources.

If the sponsor does not come to the airport or seaport to meet their visitor, they should at least be at the end of the phone, so that they can be telephoned if queries arise.

Unfortunately, there's no right of appeal against being refused entry as a visitor, whatever the reasons given.

Length of visits

Until 1 October 1994, the immigration rules said that visitors who were allowed in would be admitted for six months automatically, even if they were only intending to stay for a few days. However, in 1994 the rules changed, and now visitors can be admitted for *up to* six months, provided they do not work – so people may be admitted for rather less. Asking for the full six months could be taken to suggest that you want to stay longer than a 'normal' visit.

A visitor arriving in the UK will have their passport stamped by the Immigration Officer, showing the date and the port at which they entered. It's the date on the passport stamp that shows how long the person can stay, not the entry clearance date. Sometimes people are admitted for less than six months – this could indicate that the Immigration Officer is suspicious of their intentions.

Illegal entrants and overstayers

'Illegal entrants' are people who have entered (or tried to enter) the UK unlawfully. 'Overstayers' are people who have entered legally but then outstayed their permission to be here. In the language used by the Home Office, an illegal entrant can be 'removed', if caught, while an overstayer is 'deported'; but in both cases the person must leave the UK. People who have broken the rules in connection with their stay (they are 'in breach of their conditions of entry') can also be deported.

Of the various types of illegal entry, **entry without leave to enter** covers people who evade immigration control, perhaps by coming by boat to a port where there isn't any. More problematically, it *also* covers people who do go through immigration controls but are not given formal leave to enter.

> In one case, two people were mistakenly treated as British citizens by the Immigration Officer, and told to pass through without any stamp being placed in their passports. It was decided that they were illegal entrants and could be removed from the UK.

It's for the Immigration Officer to prove that someone is in fact an illegal entrant, but this is not difficult when they should have a stamp in their passport but do not.

Entry by deception is when a person obtains entry clearance, or permission to enter the UK at the port of entry, by making a false statement or representation. But the 'leave' or permission obtained remains valid until the decision is taken to treat that individual as an illegal entrant and remove them from the UK.

A representation is 'false' if you know or believe it to be untrue, and it must be important ('material') to the decision to give you leave to enter. You are not duty bound to volunteer information you are not asked for, but in some cases keeping silent can amount to deception. If you entered with false documents, you can be treated as an illegal entrant even if you are not aware that they are false (for instance, if you cannot read and write, and therefore do not know that a passport is not yours).

Someone who is to be removed as an illegal entrant is given a written notice of the fact, and directions are made for removal to a particular country. There is sometimes a delay between the decision and the actual removal, and people can be detained during that time. Appeals against removal generally have to take place after the person has left the UK.

Overstayers, who remain here after their limited leave has expired, are liable to be deported. If people have applied for an extension of their limited leave before it expires, they do not become overstayers while the application is being considered, because leave is automatically extended until 28 days after the Home Office decision on the application.

Since 8 November 1996, someone who **breaks a condition** about 'recourse to public funds' (explained on p 26) can be liable for deportation as a result.

Even if someone is liable to be deported, there has to be a formal decision whether to make a deportation order against them. The public interest in favour of deportation is supposed to be balanced against compassionate circumstances such as a person's age, length of residence in the UK, and their good character. There has been an assumption in the past that a deportation order would not be made once someone had had 14 years' continuous lawful or unlawful residence in the UK, since it was Home Office policy to grant indefinite leave to remain after this period. But if a deportation order was made earlier, even if the person was not aware of it, it can be carried out many years later.

There are rights of appeal under the Immigration Act, but they are very restricted if the deportation is on grounds of overstaying or breach of conditions, and if the person has been in the UK for less than seven years.

Repatriation

Under Section 29 of the Immigration Act 1971, the Government funds a small humanitarian programme that provides assistance for non-British citizens who wish to return to their countries of origin but who lack sufficient means to do so. Assistance is limited to help with fares and incidental expenses including transport of a small amount of personal possessions. The programme is administered on behalf of the Home Office by the International Social Services of Great Britain (see 'Useful addresses', p 118).

Refugees and asylum seekers

Under international law and conventions, people fleeing persecution in their own country have the right to seek asylum in other countries. The 1951 United Nations Convention Relating to the Status of Refugees defines a **refugee** as someone who has 'a well-founded fear of persecution for reasons of race, religion, nationality, membership of a particular social group or political opinion'.

This book does not cover the details of applying for and obtaining refugee status, which needs specialist advice. Contact the Refugee Legal Centre (address on p 119) or a local law centre for help.

An **asylum seeker** is someone who is claiming refugee status, but who has not yet received a final decision.

The UK is a signatory to the UN Convention, but it has increasingly tightened its policy regarding refugees and asylum seekers. The 1993 Asylum and Immigration Appeals Act, and changes in the procedures following on from this, restricted the Home Office consideration of asylum applications but clarified the rules on appeals against refusals. The 1996 Asylum and Immigration Act made further changes, but there is still a right of appeal in all cases where refusal of asylum would mean removal to a country where that person has claimed they fear persecution. People who are not granted refugee status can be granted 'exceptional leave to remain' if there are humanitarian reasons. Although the proportion of applicants granted refugee status has remained roughly constant over recent years, the proportion granted exceptional leave to remain has dropped considerably.

Over the 18 months before the passing of the Asylum and Immigration Appeals Act in 1993, only 16 per cent of decisions were outright refusals. In the 12 months after the Act came into force, 74 per cent of decisions were refusals, according to the Refugee Council. (Rights of appeal against the refusal of refugee status are covered on p 36.)

If someone applies for asylum when they arrive at an airport or port in the UK, they will be interviewed briefly by the Immigration Service to establish basic details, and fingerprinted. If the Immigration officers are satisfied that the application should be considered in the UK, the person will either be granted temporary admission to live at a named address or be detained. They will also be given a Standard Acknowledgement Letter (SAL1) to use as proof of identity, and a form IS96 confirming that they have been granted temporary admission. In due course, they will be called back to the airport or port for interview, and the details then sent to the Home Office for a decision.

A person applying for asylum when already in the UK will normally be sent a Gen32 form, asking them to go for interview at the Home Office's Screening Unit in Croydon. They will then be given a standard acknowledgement letter (SAL2).

There may be a long delay before the decision is reached. Meanwhile the person is legally in the UK but without any sort of special rights, and without access to Social Security, as explained in Chapter 8.

On receiving an application for asylum, the authorities may grant leave to stay in the UK in one of the following two ways.

Refugee status

A person who is granted refugee status is initially given permission to remain in the UK for four years. Dependent family members who are with them at the time are also given the same status. At the end of that time, she or he can apply for permanent settlement. Anyone with full refugee status is eligible to be joined in the UK by his or her spouse (so long as the marriage took place before being granted refugee status) and by dependent children (that is, children under 18). It is not necessary to demonstrate the need to maintain these family members without 'recourse to public funds' (explained in Chapter 7). But they are not eligible to be joined by other family members such as parents, though it may be possible if there are very strong compassionate circumstances.

'Exceptional leave to remain'

A much larger proportion of people applying for refugee status are instead granted 'exceptional leave to remain'. This is outside the normal immigration rules, and it is usually given for only one year to start with. This can then be renewed. Standard practice is to grant two further periods of three years each, and only then – after seven years altogether – can indefinite leave to remain be considered.

The Home Office will usually consider allowing family members to join a person with exceptional leave to remain in the UK only after their *fourth* year with that status. In exceptionally compassionate circumstances, however, they may consider applications made earlier.

In fact, because of delays in the system, an application can take considerably longer. The person must also show that they can maintain the family member(s) with 'no recourse to public funds' (see Chapter 7).

> **Note** The rules on Social Security benefits for asylum seekers were altered, and made far more restrictive, in February 1996. These are covered in Chapter 5.

Appealing against immigration decisions

There is a system of appeals against decisions of the Immigration Service and the Home Office. However, not every decision can be appealed against – there's no right of appeal against being refused entry as a visitor, for example.

There's a two-tier judicial body, independent of the Home Office. Appeals are heard first by an **adjudicator**, who decides cases on his or her own. The losing side then has the right to appeal to the **Immigration Appeals Tribunal**, which can review the case and grant 'leave to appeal' if the three members of the tribunal think there is an important legal point involved. The table on the next page, taken from the *Immigration and Nationality Law Handbook*, summarises when and where you must appeal, and how long you have to do so.

There is a separate asylum appeals system, set up under the Asylum and Immigration Appeals Act 1993, as explained on page 36.

Appealing about entry clearance or extension of time

If entry clearance is refused by a British High Commission or Embassy, there may be a right of appeal within three months of the decision. However, if someone has been refused clearance because of a 'mandatory' requirement, such as not having the right documents or not being in the right age group, or if they are applying to come as a visitor, there is no right of appeal.

Immigration appeals and time limits

Decision	Notes	Time limit to appeal to adjudicator	Time limit to apply to tribunal
Refusal of entry clearance/visa	Appellant outside UK	3 months	42 days
Refusal of entry to UK	Appellant in UK if had visa/entry clearance	28 days	14 days
	Appellant outside UK if no visa/entry clearance	28 days	42 days
Refusal to vary or extend leave to remain	Appellant in UK if applied in time	14 days	14 days
	If applied late/'out of time'	No appeal ————————	
Decision to deport	Full appeal if in UK over 7 years	14 days	14 days
	On facts of case only, if in UK less than 7 years	14 days	14 days
–on national security grounds	No appeal – review by panel only ————————		
Court recommendation for deportation	Appeal through courts system only ————————		
Deportation order signed	Only against destination	14 days	14 days
Removal as illegal entrant	Appellant in UK, only on identity grounds	28 days	14 days
	After removal	28 days	42 days
Refusal to revoke deportation order	Appellant outside UK	28 days	42 days

Source: *Immigration and Nationality Handbook*

If you have arrived in the UK with entry clearance and are then refused, you have the right to appeal within 28 days, and can remain in the UK while the appeal is heard (which could be many months). If you have arrived without entry clearance, you still have the right to appeal within 28 days, but you must go back to the country from which you came before you can exercise it.

If you have applied to extend or vary your stay in the UK and been turned down, you have 14 days in which to lodge an appeal. But you lose the right to appeal if you did not make the original application until after your permission to stay had run out, or if you are asking for a period of stay longer than that allowed by the immigration rules.

Forms and time limits

Anyone who is refused entry is given notice of the decision in a standard printed letter. The authorities also send copies of the appeal forms to be filled in, advising the time limits, and a note of the addresses to which the forms must be sent. You *must* use the right forms, available from the Home Office Application Forms Unit (address on p 118), and send all the documents listed in them. The time limits are extremely important – if you do not stick to them, you can lose your right of appeal. There is no need to fill in the section headed 'Grounds of appeal' in detail, if there is no time to obtain proper advice. Put instead 'The decision is not in accordance with the immigration law and rules applicable. Further grounds will follow.'

Once an appeal has been lodged, the Home Office should send an *acknowledgement letter*, which supersedes the refusal letter and allows you to stay until the appeal is heard.

Appeals to the Adjudicator are often decided on the papers supplied, but you can also opt to have an oral appeal if you prefer. It can be rather an ordeal, but it could be a good idea if your case depends on the credibility of your story, and you feel you could convince someone face to face.

If you lose the appeal to the Adjudicator, you have a right to go further, to the Immigration Appeals Tribunal, which is rather more formal. You can also take an appeal to the courts if there is an important point of law involved.

Appealing in asylum cases

If your appeal is against being refused asylum, there is a separate system of 'special adjudicators' and (in some cases) also the Immigration Appeals Tribunal. The time limits, though, are much shorter, and there is a special 'fast track' for appeals about cases that the Home Office says are 'without foundation'. These are mainly cases where people have fled via a third country, and could have claimed asylum there. They can be removed to that country if the Home Office considers that that country is 'safe'. If they have been refused asylum personally at the port of entry, someone whose case is certified as 'without foundation' is given just two working days in which to make an appeal to the Adjudicator. There is no further right of appeal to the Tribunal.

Other people have ten days in which to appeal to the Adjudicator, and then five days to go to the Tribunal if necessary.

Advice and representation

It is important to get advice and help with preparing your case, from specialists if you are pursuing an appeal. The refusal letter gives you details of two organisations to consult: the Immigration Advisory Service or the Refugee Legal Centre (see 'Useful addresses', p 117). You could also go to a local law centre, or ask the Citizens Advice Bureau to refer you to a solicitor who specialises in that area.

4 Returning residents and immigration controls

The position of someone who has left the UK once, and wants to come back again, depends on whether or not they have 'settled status', as defined in the Immigration Act 1971. Effectively, anyone who is ordinarily resident and has indefinite leave to enter or remain is 'settled' in the UK.

Ordinary residence has a special meaning. It is not the same as your **domicile** (explained in the Glossary, p 99), which depends partly on your state of mind. You can be ordinarily resident in two countries at the same time. The term 'ordinary residence' refers, according to a 1983 case in the House of Lords, to your residence in a particular place which you have adopted voluntarily and for settled purposes as part of the regular order of your life for the time being, whether of short or long duration. The residence must be for a settled purpose or purposes, even if you do not intend to stay indefinitely. Occasional absences abroad do not necessarily break the ordinary residence; this will always need to be decided on the facts of each particular case. There has to be some degree of continuity, but you cannot include as part of ordinary residence any period of unlawful residence or presence.

People returning to the UK from overseas are to be admitted, according to the rules, if;

- they had indefinite leave to enter or remain in the UK when they last left; and
- they have not been away for longer than two years; and
- they now seek admission for the purpose of settlement.

Anyone who received help from public funds to leave the country originally (such as a repatriation grant – see p 30) is not covered by this rule.

British Overseas citizens who hold UK passports and have been admitted once for settlement in the UK since 1 March 1968 have a right to be readmitted for settlement. This means that, even if they stay away from the UK for more than two years at a time, they cannot be refused indefinite leave to remain when they return.

If other people left more than two years ago, they can still ask for admission as returning residents, though they do not have this as an automatic right. But the rules say that they should be admitted if, for example, they have spent most of their lives in the UK. Other factors that will be taken into account include:

- the reasons that the absence has been longer than two years;
- whether this was their own decision or through no fault of their own (because they fell sick, for instance);
- their purpose and intent in returning at this time;
- the nature of their family ties, how close they are and how far they have maintained them while out of the country; and
- whether they still have a home in this country and intend to continue living in it.

In general, the longer the period someone has been abroad, the more difficult it will be to requalify. You don't need a visa if you are returning to the UK within two years.

Note In terms of claiming benefits, the 'habitual residence' test (explained on pp 70–73) has created much tighter restrictions than in the past. This means that some settled and British people will no longer qualify for Income Support, Housing Benefit or Council Tax Benefit. Check those rules, and your Social Security position generally, before taking any decisions about going abroad or returning to the UK.

---

5 | Social Security and people from other countries

Broadly speaking, British Social Security benefits are divided into two main groups: those to which you have a right provided you fulfil certain conditions, but regardless of your income; and those that are means-tested – that is, whether you can have them depends first on fulfilling the conditions and then *also* on how little income or capital you have. Some, such as retirement pensions, widows' pensions and incapacity benefits, are **contributory**. This means that, before it can even be decided whether you qualify, you have to have made the right number of National Insurance contributions (or their equivalent in certain other countries). Others, such as Attendance Allowance and Invalid Care Allowance, are **non-contributory**, but still depend on your meeting certain conditions (including, now, a right to reside permanently in the UK, as explained on pp 64–65).

In order to receive one of the **means-tested benefits**, you must have less than a certain amount of capital and income, in relation to your family size. These include Income Support and Family Credit, Housing Benefit and Council Tax Benefit. There is also some help available with National Health Service charges and prescriptions if you are on a low income, as explained on page 89.

This book gives only a broad outline of the various benefits covered. For more detail, and for information about those not covered, look in *Your Rights*, published annually by Age Concern England, and in the publications by CPAG listed in 'Useful publications' (p 121).

What counts as the UK?

Technically, the rules explained in this book apply only to Great Britain. Great Britain consists of England, Wales and Scotland; it does *not* include Northern Ireland, the Isle of Man or the Channel Islands, which have their own Social Security legislation. The United Kingdom does include Northern Ireland.

However, because of the close links between Great Britain, Northern Ireland and the Isle of Man, you will not lose any benefit by moving between them. National Insurance contributions paid in one of these counts as though they were paid in any of the others. So for most practical purposes, the systems in Great Britain, Northern Ireland and the Isle of Man can be treated as identical. So I have referred in this part of the book to the 'United Kingdom' or UK, as that is the phrase people most often use, even though it's not technically quite correct. If the situation is different with a particular rule, I have said so.

The Channel Islands have their own Social Security system but with a reciprocal agreement (explained on p 48) under which you can receive British benefits while there.

For practical purposes, 'abroad' or 'overseas' in this book therefore means everywhere that is not the Isle of Man, one of the Channel Islands or part of the UK.

How Social Security is administered

Most of the different benefits are administered by the Benefits Agency, part of the Department of Social Security (DSS), which has offices throughout the UK. National Insurance contributions are dealt with by the Contributions Agency, which has a section called International Services dealing with contribution questions for people under pension age where there is an overseas issue. There is a specialist section of the Benefits Agency, the Pensions and Overseas Benefits Directorate (POD), which deals with National Insurance questions relating to pensions and for people who have come into or left the UK. There are specialists dealing with the various disability benefits. Income Support and other means-tested benefits are dealt with at the level of the local office, on the basis of detailed instructions from the centre. This will mean that staff in some local offices will be much more experienced than others in dealing with members of ethnic minority groups.

The Benefits Agency have an Equal Opportunities Policy Statement which says that:

'BA aims to be an organisation which:

- provides equal access to its services to all groups of people;
- establishes a reputation as a good service provider to ethnic minority groups; and
- represents, at all grades, the community we serve to help meet the needs of our customers.'

Their Customer Services Charter recognises that some customers have particular needs. This includes people with disabilities and those from ethnic minorities. The Charter says that BA staff will listen and respond to these customers and their representative organisations.

Housing Benefit is dealt with by local councils, most of which should have a similar charter or equal opportunities statement. War Pensions (covered in Chapter 11) are dealt with by a separate Agency within the DSS (address on p 95).

Making a claim

For almost every benefit, you have to make a claim, and you only become entitled to benefits when you do so. The claim must usually be in writing; it should be on the proper form, though if you send in a letter instead the Secretary of State has the power to treat it as a valid claim.

There are strict time limits for claims. For retirement pension, widows' benefits, Incapacity Benefit and Severe Disablement Allowance, you need to claim within three months (soon to become only one month) if you are not to lose some of the benefits. So long as you keep within these time limits, the benefit can be backdated to the date when you became eligible. The Benefits Agency can accept a late claim only in very limited circumstances. For Disability Living Allowance and Attendance Allowance, a claim cannot be backdated to before the date on which it is claimed.

Maria has been living in Canada for ten years, and when she reaches 60 someone tells her she may be entitled to some UK retirement pension. She does not get around to writing until two months later, but she can then receive full arrears back to the date when she was 60, because this is less than three months ago.

Albert hears about her success and decides to write also. But he is already aged 68, and so reached British state pension age three years ago. He can receive backdated pension for the last three months, but has lost out on more than two years' benefit by not claiming before. He will, though, receive a higher pension once he starts claiming, as it will have been accumulating 'increments' at the rate of 1 per cent for every 7 weeks it has been waiting to be claimed.

So the answer is *always* to put in a claim if you think you might be entitled to benefit; you have nothing to lose by doing so, and will gain if you are right.

If you are in the UK, you can claim by contacting the local Benefits Agency office (the address should be in the phone directory). If the claim raises questions that need to be referred to POD, the local office will start a file but then refer the case on. Alternatively, or if you are living in another country, you can write directly to POD (address on p 117). When they respond, you will be given the name of the person who is dealing with your case (and their direct phone number), and you can contact them direct. They can phone you back if you ring them from abroad, and they also have an answerphone system to take account of the different time zones.

When you make a claim, give as much information as you can in order to help them trace your record. Your National Insurance number is the most important, but your current and past addresses, date of birth and any names by which you or your spouse may have been known in the past will be useful. Keep copies of any documents you send them.

There are also specialist Pensions Liaison Officers in Dhaka and Islamabad. These are the only people employed by the DSS in the Indian sub-continent to help people with their claims. Much of their time, as explained below, is spent checking claims against the Entry Clearance records, but they can also help people with making an initial claim, for instance by filling in the form. Staff at the British Embassy or High Commission in other countries should also have supplies of the relevant forms, and the leaflets about any reciprocal agreements (listed on pp 114–115) that apply to that country.

Many people making claims from other countries go through agents or local solicitors, to whom they may well have to pay a fee. This will usually be a waste of money, at least at the first stages. POD will ask you for the relevant information, and give you a ruling on which you can then appeal if necessary.

If you feel a decision is wrong

Most Social Security decisions are made by Adjudication Officers (AOs). If you disagree with one of their decisions, you have a right to ask for it to be reviewed, or to make an appeal to a Social Security Appeal Tribunal (SSAT). There are also some decisions that are officially taken by the Secretary of State (explained below).

When you are told about whether you have been awarded a benefit and how much you will get, you should also be told what to do if you disagree with the decision. If you want to challenge this, it is often useful to ask for advice from a local agency such as the Citizens Advice Bureau. They may be able to help you write to the DSS, and prepare your case and perhaps represent you at the tribunal.

You can ask for a decision about benefits to be **reviewed** at any time, if you think the Adjudication Officer did not have all the facts or misunderstood what you told them, if your circumstances have changed, or if you think the decision is incorrect for some other reason. Write to the Benefits Agency office dealing with your case, asking for the decision to be reviewed, and giving your reasons. If your request is turned down, you can appeal against this decision.

If you want to **appeal**, get leaflet NI246, *How to Appeal*, from the Benefits Agency office and write your appeal in the tear-off form on the back of this. The form asks you to provide details of:

- the date on which you were told of the decision you are appealing against;
- the claim or issue to which the decision relates; and
- a summary of your arguments for saying that the decision is wrong.

If you have missed the time limit for appealing, you also need to give details of your special reasons for appealing late.

Your appeal must get to the local Benefits Agency office within three months of the date of your being sent notice of the decision. Get it in earlier if you can, because they then have to send it on to the Independent Tribunal Service.

If you write a letter rather than filling in the special form, the tribunal's chairperson *may* accept it as an appeal, so long as it contains all the necessary detail. But they could turn it down if you have missed something out, so it is better not to risk it.

When the Independent Tribunal Service has received your appeal, they will ask if you want an oral hearing. If you say no, or do not reply within ten days, your appeal will be decided on the basis of your written arguments and any documents you have submitted. It is usually better to say that you will attend, because the chances of winning are much greater if you can be there to put your side of the case.

In due course, you will be sent a set of all the documents relating to your case, and details of where and when the tribunal will take place. The cases are heard by three people not connected with the DSS. It is always worth turning up to the tribunal if you possibly can; if you cannot, the case may be heard in your absence. It is often best to have a representative. If you do not have a representative, it is worth taking a friend or relative to help or for moral support. You might be able to get assistance from a law centre or the Citizens Advice Bureau in putting your case. You are entitled to an interpreter.

The proceedings can be rather daunting, but they should be kept informal and you should have the time to put your case and answer questions from the tribunal members. They must then decide whether the Adjudication Officer has made the right decision according to a reasonable interpretation of the law. If the law has been followed, they cannot change a decision just because it seems unfair. You may be told the outcome straight away; otherwise, the decision will be sent to you later.

It's perfectly possible to send in an appeal from abroad (indeed, many are heard each year), but the time limits are just the same. If you can persuade a friend or a relative to represent you at the hearing, it will be helpful. There's a much higher success rate at appeals when the claimant or someone speaking for them is present, than when they are not.

Normally, an appeal is heard at the centre closest to where you live. If you are abroad but have someone to represent you, you can ask for the appeal to be heard wherever is most convenient for them. Otherwise it is heard in Newcastle upon Tyne, simply because that is the closest place to the POD office.

If you want to appeal in person, reasonable travelling expenses can be paid for travel *within the UK*, but not for travel abroad.

Secretary of State's decisions cover mainly the question of whether you have paid the right number or type of National Insurance contributions. There is no formal arrangement for appealing on these, but if you disagree you can ask for them to be reconsidered. The Secretary of State relies heavily on the computer records in the Contributions Agency. But if you can explain why you think the computer record is wrong, he or she is willing to accept that it is not perfect at times.

People who are not fluent in English

The DSS used to run a free telephone helpline, using 0800 numbers, in Chinese, Punjabi and Urdu. Sadly, however, this has now closed down along with the main DSS Freefone service, and people have to contact their local Benefits Agency offices direct. They do still provide some audio tapes and leaflets in other languages; the tape on Pensions and Retirement, for instance (ref TA3), is available in Chinese, Gujarati, Hindi, Polish, Punjabi, Somali, Sylheti, Turkish, Urdu and Vietnamese. The list of relevant DSS leaflets on pages 111–115 gives details of those available in other languages.

In July 1996, the DSS announced a new arrangement called a *Language Skills Points Card* (LSC1). The idea is that someone coming into an office who cannot speak English is shown a copy of the card (in fact, really a leaflet) on which there are the words 'I speak and understand this language' in 30 foreign languages. Once they have selected their language, they can be given a 'basic skills' (BSK1) card which can be specially amended to show their individual language needs. People will then be able to show this card when they need help to communicate. But it is not clear yet how well this system will operate in practice.

For Benefits Agency (BA) staff, there is a booklet, *Bridging the Language Barrier*, setting out the minimum requirements for the BA service to customers whose first language is not spoken English. There is also a *Good Practice Guide*, containing information about cultural awareness, interpreting and different naming systems, and a *Language Skills* directory of translation and interpreting abilities among BA staff.

People who do not speak English are free to bring with them a friend or relative to act as interpreter in any appointment with the BA. Alternatively, the BA aim to make arrangements within one working day to provide spoken interpreting services where needed. These may be provided by a member of staff, by community or commercial interpreters, or by a telephone service (called Language Line). The BA are setting up a contract to provide telephone interpreting services across the whole of the country, for use where face-to-face interpreting is not possible. Some BA areas, such as Kirklees in Yorkshire, employ bilingual staff who can both interpret and administer the benefits for their language groups.

The BA's own Code of Practice says that they should offer an interpreting service where there is a communication barrier between the customer and the BA because of a lack of a common language, and the customer indicates that they want this. The customer should always have the choice of using either an interpreter provided and paid for by BA or a person of their own choice.

Some people, the BA document says, may automatically bring someone with them to interpret, because they consider they will need their help. BA staff should explain about the range of language services available through BA, so that the customer then has the choice of whom to use. If they bring their own professional, qualified interpreter, a refund of reasonable costs can be considered at local level.

The Code of Practice says that it is *not* acceptable:

- to use minors as interpreters; or
- to send someone away to find a friend, relative or other person to act as interpreter.

Documents in a foreign language, if handed over to the BA, can be translated through their Pensions and Overseas Benefits Directorate (POD). As they can use freelance translation agencies where necessary, they are able to translate from any language.

Confusion over names

There may be confusion within the DSS about your correct name. For instance, your National Insurance contribution record and your NHS card may use different names. The officials concerned may have arrived at what they believe to be your name without having thought it out, or checked it properly with you. One result can be delay, and even non-payment of benefit.

For example, people from Spain and many Latin American countries have *two* surnames. The first is their father's and the second their mother's. In the UK, it would be assumed that the last one is the 'real' surname. In fact (except for married women) it is the second to last.

In some cultures, people will have several names and call themselves different things according to the circumstances, and this can also add to the confusion. It is usually a good idea to decide on the personal name and surname that you wish to use in official papers in the UK, and then to check that these are always used (and in the same order) in any communications with officials.

If in the past you have used different names and there has been confusion, ask for advice about what steps to take. One suggestion is that you write a formal letter to all the official bodies with whom you have been in contact, giving all the details and saying that from now on you will be known as −.

Links between the DSS and the Home Office

There are close links between the Benefits Agency and the Home Office. The Income Support claim form asks whether you, or anyone you are claiming for, has come to the UK in the last five years. If the answer is yes, you are likely to be interviewed to determine whether you, or the person you are claiming for, is a 'person from abroad' as explained in Chapter 3. You are also asked on the form about whether you came to the UK under a sponsorship undertaking (explained on p 73). You are likely to be asked to show your passport, both for this reason and for others such as verifying your age.

If your immigration status is not clear, the Benefits Agency will contact the Home Office to check. So making a claim for Income Support can alert the immigration authorities to the fact that someone is here illegally, or has broken the conditions of entry by claiming public funds.

It is best to ask for advice before claiming, especially if there have been problems in the past with your immigration status, or if you feel that the right National Insurance or tax might not have been paid in the past.

Use of Immigration Service records

Immigration Service records can also be used by the DSS to decide on benefit claims – and indeed to review claims they have accepted in the past. The DSS's own Pensions Liaison Officers in Dhaka and Islamabad, and High Commission or Embassy staff elsewhere, have access to the Entry Clearance Officer's files going back many years. If requested by the Pensions and Overseas Benefits Directorate, they will go through these files and check whether there have been previous questions raised, perhaps about the status of a marriage. They do not need your permission to do this search, as all the material will be facts that you have voluntarily told to the High Commission, and given verification for.

They may also visit the village from which a claimant or their dependant originated, and check the official records there. Any information obtained in this way, and such items as the transcripts of interviews for an entry certificate, will then be sent to the UK and reviewed by the Adjudication Officer – in some cases meaning that benefit is lost.

Reciprocal agreements

There are some countries with whom the UK has 'reciprocal agreements' on Social Security, and these are listed in Appendix 2. They are mostly countries in the industrialised West, and there are hardly any with African or Asian countries, so they are not helpful for many people in ethnic minority communities in the UK.

These agreements are fairly limited, and do not always mean that your benefits (or the annual increases in them) can be paid when you are abroad. They may only allow contributions to be added together ('aggregated'). There are leaflets available on each country from the DSS Pensions and Overseas Benefits Directorate (see p 40).

EEA countries

For countries that are members of the European Economic Area (EEA), explained on page 103, two important principles help people to qualify for certain Social Security benefits if they live or work in different EEA countries at different times in their working lives.

Aggregation

This is a rule that applies when you claim a benefit for the first time, usually after you have stopped working. It is highly complicated, but the main points are:

- you receive benefit only from the last EEA country where you were insured;
- wherever you make the claim, it is referred to the relevant Social Security institution in the country where you were last insured, and that institution calculates the benefit that is due;
- this involves treating periods of insurance or residence in other countries as though they were periods in the country where you were last insured;
- the benefit is usually paid through the relevant Social Security institution in the country where you are now living, and that institution carries out any medical examinations.

> **Rainaldo** last worked in Italy, but has now retired to the UK to be with his family. He makes his pension claim through the Benefits Agency, and will receive a benefit calculated by the Italian authorities but paid through the Benefits Agency.

'Exporting' benefits

Some (but by no means all) UK Social Security can be 'exported' if you move to another EEA country after you have started claiming the benefit. The relevant ones are:

- Jobseeker's Allowance (contribution-related)
- Incapacity Benefit (ICB)
- Severe Disablement Allowance (SDA)
- widow's benefits
- retirement pension

This means that anyone who is considered to be employed or self-employed, who starts receiving one of these benefits and then moves to another country within the EEA can continue to receive it there. You are counted as 'employed or self-employed' if you are currently insured under a national Social Security scheme (that is, you either pay National Insurance contributions or ought to do so as an employed or self-employed person) or if you are receiving a benefit covered by the rules on the basis of contributions paid in the past.

In general, people who are receiving Incapacity Benefit, retirement pensions or widow's pensions will be covered by this rule, because they would not be getting the benefit unless they had made such contributions. So they can then travel anywhere within the EEA without losing their benefits, so long as they continue to satisfy all the conditions of entitlement except residence. People claiming Severe Disablement Allowance are much less likely to be covered, unless they are travelling with family members who are classified as 'workers'.

The *other* disability benefits, such as Disability Living Allowance and Attendance Allowance, are not covered by this rule. Nor are any of the means-tested benefits. So it is important to check before leaving the UK what effect these rules will have on your income. See DSS leaflet NI 38, *Social Security Abroad,* for further information.

6 National Insurance contributory benefits

As explained in the last chapter, some Social Security benefits are classed as **contributory**, and paid out of the National Insurance Fund. Whether you are eligible for these at all (assuming you meet the other conditions) depends on whether the right sort of National Insurance contributions have been paid, at the right time. The benefits considered in this chapter are:

State retirement pensions (basic and additional);
State widows' pensions;
Incapacity Benefit (for people too sick to work).

> **Note** Only brief details of the benefits themselves are given here. For fuller information, refer to *Your Rights*, published annually by Age Concern (details on p 121), and the various DSS leaflets referred to below.

State basic retirement pensions

To qualify for a state retirement pension, you must have reached pension age (currently 65 for men and 60 for women, though it is changing in future for women born after 6 April 1950). You must also fulfil the National Insurance (NI) contribution conditions.

Whenever you are working and earning more than a certain amount each week, you should have NI contributions deducted from your pay and passed to the DSS, or should be paying them yourself if you are self-employed. Records are kept throughout your working life, both of what you have paid and of 'credits' given for periods when you could not work. There are two conditions that you must meet in order to receive a pension.

First, you must have paid enough contributions during at least one year in your working life since 6 April 1975, or paid at least 50 flat-rate contributions (the old system before that date) before 6 April 1975.

Secondly, to receive a full basic retirement pension you must have paid or been credited with contributions for about nine-tenths of your 'working life' (explained below). To receive any basic pension at all you must have a minimum number of years' contributions or credits, for about a quarter of your 'working life'.

Your 'working life' is the period over which you have to meet the contribution conditions for basic retirement pension – normally 44 years for a woman and 49 years for a man. It is counted from the start of the tax year in which you reach 16 to the end of the tax year before the one in which you reach pensionable age, whether you were in the UK or not at that age. Even if you work abroad and then return to the UK, your working life will go back to age 16.

But if you were over 16 when the National Insurance scheme started on 5 July 1948, your working life will depend on whether you were already insured for pension purposes at 5 July 1948. Under the scheme that existed before that date, not all employment was insurable nor was insurance necessarily continuous.

If you were already insured for pension purposes on 5 July 1948, your working life will start on the latest of these dates:

- at the beginning of the tax year in which you last entered the National Insurance scheme; or
- 6 April 1936.

If you were not insured for pension purposes on 5 July 1948, your working life started on 6 April 1948.

So someone who came to the UK later in life may have a gap in his or her contribution record, and so be unable to earn a full pension.

> **Ismail** came to the UK as an adult, when he was 25, and started working and paying National Insurance contributions immediately. But when he comes to retire at 65, he finds he has paid for only 40 years out of 49. To get a full pension, he would need to have paid for at least 44. Instead, he receives 91 per cent of the full amount, and 91 per cent of any later increases.

The reciprocal agreements (explained on p 48) and the special rules for EEA member countries (explained on pp 49–50) will help some people to qualify for benefit, if they had previously been working in a country whose contributions can be 'aggregated' with the UK's. In general, you will get a pension that is proportional to the part of your working life you have spent in each country. So you might end up with a total pension that is higher than if you had been in the UK alone, but not with two (or more) full pensions.

The retirement pension claim form asks for details of insurance in other countries. The Benefits Agency will then be responsible for sorting out the calculations as between different countries, but there can be some delays.

Because retirement ages differ between countries, you may be able to draw a pension (or part of one) from another country earlier than you can draw the British retirement pension, or it might only arise later. The benefits will be adjusted under the 'proportional' arrangement explained above if a new benefit becomes payable.

It is your responsibility to pursue any non-UK pensions that would be payable before the UK one. Some countries also require you to send in evidence every so often that you are still alive. Contact your local DSS office to arrange this.

Proving your age

For some people, it will be difficult to prove their age because they have come from a country where birth certificates are not universal or not reliable, or because the records have been lost in wars or other upheavals. It's your responsibility to prove your age, but the DSS should help you in searching for evidence.

Often, your passport is the only document you have that gives your age. If it is given as a year or a month rather than an actual date, the DSS assume your birthday to be the *least* beneficial date for you. This will normally be the last day of the year or month. So if your birth date is given as '1939', when you apply for a pension it will be assumed that your birthday was on 31 December and you cannot therefore qualify any earlier.

Once the DSS have decided on a birth date at the beginning or end of a particular month or year, they use it in all subsequent benefit claims. But if you can produce new evidence that shows an earlier or later date of birth, the DSS should review their earlier decision and pay any arrears that are due.

If there's uncertainty about the *year* of your birth, the DSS can accept all sorts of 'secondary records' as well as a birth certificate. Examples of documents they have accepted include:

- army records;
- baptism or other religious certificate;
- school records (such as school reports);
- health records or medical assessments of your age; driving licence; alien's identity book or naturalisation certificate (but this normally has to be supported by something else, as you could simply have made a personal statement about your age at the time when you registered if it was some time ago);
- statements from people who know you and your family;
- deductions from the proven age of brothers or sisters, or other relatives.

If there's no other evidence, your own statement should be accepted unless it is contradictory or improbable. (Evidence from immigration records could be used to disprove it, if you have given a different age previously.) You have a right of appeal if the DSS refuse to accept your statement.

Increases for dependants

A married woman who has worked and paid full contributions all her life will be entitled to a state basic pension in her own right, and there are some special arrangements (called Home Responsibility Protection) when she has taken time away from work to look after children or other dependants.

If she is under the age of 60 when her husband claims retirement pension, he could be entitled to Adult Dependency Allowance, provided he makes a valid claim and supplies the right documents. If she is 60 or over, she will be able to claim a retirement pension based on his National Insurance contribution (normally 60 per cent of his basic pension). If she is only partly entitled in her own right and partly through her husband's contributions, these will be 'aggregated' to the maximum married women's rate (at April 1997 this is £37.35). If, however, her own entitlement is higher than this, her rate of pension will continue to be paid.

So a wife who may never have been to the UK, or who has only arrived after retirement age or indeed after her husband's death, could be entitled to a pension on the basis of his contributions. It is almost always worth checking. Some people will not have documentary evidence of their marriage. For benefit purposes, it is presumed that a man and woman who are living together as husband and wife are married to each other, unless there is clear contradictory evidence to which the benefits authority can point.

Is your marriage considered valid?

Broadly speaking, if a marriage is legally recognised and valid in the country in which it took place, it will be recognised as valid under UK marriage law. Whether a particular form of marriage is valid will depend on the laws of the country in which it took place, and the couple's domicile. For example, a Nigerian customary marriage, where there is no documentation and the ceremony is an exchange of gifts between the families, will be valid if it took place in Nigeria between two people both with domicile in Nigeria – but not if it takes place in the UK.

Domicile means:

> 'the country to which people feel they belong and in which they intend to spend the rest of their life. Normally people are considered to have a 'domicile of origin', usually the country in which they were born and grew up. This can only be changed by a conscious decision to settle and stay in another country and thus acquire a "domicile of choice". Questions asked to determine the domicile of people who have left their countries of origin often include where they hope to die and be buried/cremated . . . People's immigration status has no direct connection with their domicile.'
> (Source: *Immigration and Nationality Law Handbook*)

UK Social Security law usually follows the marriage law explained above, but there is an exception for a **polygamous** marriage, which is defined as one where the law of the country where it is celebrated allows either party to have another wife or husband. (Usually it is the husband who is allowed to have more than one wife, but the rules do apply in the same way if the wife is permitted two or more husbands (polyandry).)

For entitlement to Social Security benefits, the vital question is whether or not the husband or wife actually has another spouse at the date on which the claim is made for an increase (or the date of the husband's death, in the case of the widow's pension). If they have, no one receives a pension on the basis of the husband or wife's contributions. The marriage is treated as being monogamous on any day when it is *potentially* polygamous (that is, if neither husband or wife has ever had more than one spouse), or when it is *formerly polygamous* (that is, if the husband or wife has had other spouses in the past, but they have died or been divorced). But it is not treated as monogamous on any day when it is *actually polygamous*, and this can bar a spouse from receiving benefit. So a woman could be refused a dependant's pension, or a pension on the basis of her husband's contributions. It's never possible for two widows' pensions to be paid for the same husband.

> **Shaheen** has been married to her husband in Pakistan for 30 years. Five years ago he took a second wife without divorcing Shaheen. He came to the UK 12 months ago and has now reached state retirement age. Because the marriage is actually polygamous, neither wife can receive a pension based on his contributions.

> **Fara** is her husband's second wife. When he married her, he was also married to Benazir. But after a few years he divorced Benazir. This means that at the date when he reaches retirement age, Fara is the only wife, and she can receive a pension based on his contributions.

However, the law is complicated and it will be worth taking advice. If people have chosen to make the UK their permanent home, this country may then have become their *domicile*, and/or that of their spouse, in legal terms. Once someone is domiciled in the UK, she or he is not allowed to contract a polygamous marriage anywhere in the world, even if it is allowed under local law.

Johura and her husband **Tobarak** were married in Pakistan before entering the UK. After they had lived in Cardiff for many years, Tobarak went back to Pakistan and married a second wife, Jamila. But because Tobarak's domicile was now Wales, that marriage could not be valid in the UK and so Johura remained his only wife, and is able to draw her pension based on his National Insurance contributions.

If someone is claiming that a marriage was or became monogamous because a previous wife (or husband) was divorced, the DSS will investigate whether the divorce was valid. Under the Muslim Family Laws Ordinance in Pakistan, for instance, a *talaq* divorce is not effective until 90 days after a formal written notice has been delivered to the Chairman of the local Arbitration Council. So the Benefits Agency will require to see a copy of such a notice; if the Benefits Agency are not shown such a notice, they will consider that the marriage continues in force. This is the sort of question for which the Pensions Liaison Office and Foreign Office staff are used, as explained on page 48.

The Benefits Agency have a special section called the Validity of Marriages Unit (not usually mentioned to claimants). Adjudication Officers refer to this section questions about whether marriages are to be treated as monogamous. You have a right to appeal if you feel the decision is wrong.

Making a claim for retirement pension

Normally, you are sent a claim form for retirement pension about four months before you are due to reach state retirement age. If you are abroad when your claim is due, and the Benefits Agency know where to contact you, they will send the form to you there. But if you do not receive it, contact the local Benefits Agency (in the UK) or the DSS Pensions and Overseas Benefits Directorate (if you are abroad) and ask for one.

If you go abroad

There's no residence qualification for a UK pension, so you can continue to receive it if you go abroad for a short or long time (though you may not receive any increases, as explained below).

You continue to have the choice of being paid by order book or by a direct payment into a bank or building society account. If you are paid by weekly order book, you must cash each order within *three months* of the date printed on it, and they cannot be cashed abroad. Alternatives are to tell your Benefits Agency office that you will be away, and arrange for the pension to build up and be paid in one lump sum when you return, or arrange for someone else to cash your orders in the UK.

If you are not paid by weekly order book, you do not need to tell the local Benefits Agency office unless you are staying abroad for more than six months. You can, if you prefer, arrange to receive your pension in the country where you are staying. The Benefits Agency have arrangements with the Royal Bank of Scotland to convert the payments into the foreign currencies required, so you do not incur any additional costs for doing this. But there is, of course, always a risk that the currency will alter its value compared to the pound sterling, so you could find that you have less (or more) than you expect to live on.

Pension increases

If you are moving to another country in the EEA (for instance, retiring to the seaside in Spain), you will receive the annual pension increases at the same time as people in the UK. But with other countries, what matters is whether the UK has a special 'reciprocal agreement' with them (see p 48). Some of the countries with a large number of UK pensioners living there, such as Australia, Canada and the countries of the Indian sub-continent, do not have this sort of agreement. So if you are receiving retirement pension or widow's pension and you move to one of these countries, your pension will stay at the same rate as it was when you left the UK.

If you come back to the UK, you can start receiving the pension at the full rate currently in force at the time, but it will be frozen again if you leave again.

For more information, see Social Security leaflet NI 105 (payments into bank or building society accounts); or contact your local Benefits Agency office or the Pensions and Overseas Benefits Directorate (address on p 117).

Over-80s pension

This is a non-contributory retirement pension, at a lower rate than the full one (£37.35 a week instead of £62.45 in 1997/8) for people who are over the age of 80 and who do not get a retirement pension otherwise. You can receive it even if you have never paid any National Insurance contributions in Great Britain, but instead there are strict residence conditions.

To qualify, you must be living in the UK on the day you become 80, or on the day you claim, and to have been here for ten years or more in any 20-year period after your 60th birthday. Periods of residence in EEA countries will count towards this. But you can lose this benefit if you go outside the EEA or countries with a reciprocal agreement for more than six months, or even if you are away for a shorter period if you are no longer technically 'resident'. (The meaning of 'residence' in this context is explained on p 64.)

Other pensions

The State Earnings Related Pension Scheme (SERPS) generally follows the same rules as the basic pension. The old Graduated Pension (which stopped building up in 1975) is not included in the special EEA calculation arrangements, but is paid on top of any other pension you are receiving from the UK or another EEA country. Pensions from employers' pension schemes, and personal pensions from insurance companies, can normally be paid abroad, but you will have to make the claim and to arrange for an account into which the pension can be paid. You will need to be able to provide details of when and where you worked for the company in the UK.

Widows' pensions

Widows' pensions are payable provided the husband has paid enough National Insurance contributions under the same rules as for retirement pensions (explained above). The same rules apply to the retirement pension that is payable if a widow is over state retirement age (60 at present). See *Your Rights* for a full explanation of the conditions for widows' pensions.

As with the retirement pension, widows' pensions can be paid to spouses abroad. It is an 'exportable' benefit under EEA rules (see p 49), and covered by most of the reciprocal agreements to some extent. For people in countries outside the EEA or the reciprocal agreements that cover this point, the benefits will be paid but annual increases will not.

The Benefits Agency will check on the validity of the marriage if they have any doubts. For polygamous marriages (defined on pp 55–57) what matters is whether there was another wife on the *day* the husband died. If there was, no one gets a widow's pension. Many private (employers') pension schemes will follow the same rules.

Incapacity Benefit

This is the Social Security benefit paid if you are too sick to work. The contribution requirements are different from those for pensions. The rules about payment abroad are also different, and have recently been changed.

Before you can be eligible for Incapacity Benefit, you must have paid National Insurance contributions on a certain level of earnings in one contribution year (in 1997/8 the earnings figure is £1,550), and have paid or been credited with sufficient contributions in each of the last two contribution years. (There are, though, some complicated rules which mean that credited contributions do not always help you qualify for benefit.) So you may qualify only if you have spent all or most of the last two years in the UK, or possibly in another country of the EEA from which contributions can be 'aggregated', as explained on page 49.

To receive the long-term rate of Incapacity Benefit, you must then either be considered incapable of all work under the rules that are now applied or be in an exempt group – for example, suffering from one of a specific list of illnesses. See *Your Rights* for a full explanation of the conditions for Incapacity Benefit.

Going abroad with Incapacity Benefit

The rules here differ depending on how long you are away from the UK, and whether you are going to an EEA country, one with a reciprocal agreement, or elsewhere.

Incapacity Benefit is an 'exportable' benefit within the EEA. This is means that, once you are receiving Incapacity Benefit, you can travel to another EEA country without losing it so long as you still qualify under the other rules. The other country will be responsible for carrying out medical examinations as necessary. These vary enormously in quality across countries; the standard German examination, for instance, can take up to two hours and is much more thorough than the UK's equivalent.

Most (but not all) of the reciprocal agreements with other countries outside the EEA cover Incapacity Benefit, but their provisions may be fairly limited. Get the relevant leaflet (see list on pp 111–116) from the Pensions and Overseas Benefits Directorate before you leave.

The 26-week rule

Once you are receiving Incapacity Benefit, you can go to other countries not in the EEA or covered by reciprocal agreements, and still receive it for a temporary absence of up to 26 weeks (six months), but only if the Secretary of State will certify that paying it would be 'consistent with the proper administration of the Act' *and either*:

1 your absence from Great Britain is for the specific purpose of being treated for an illness which began before you left this country;

   or

2 when you left this country you had been continuously incapable of work for six months, and you have been continuously incapable of work since your departure.

The courts and the Social Security Commissioners have taken some rather confusing decisions on what 'temporary' means in this context – they have now said that it depends on the circumstances of each individual case. A 'temporary absence' does not have to mean you have a fixed date for your return, but it must nevertheless be for a limited period only.

The decision on whether to give a certificate or not is technically one for the Secretary of State, though in practice it will be the civil servants in the local office who take it. In most cases, there will be few problems over a short holiday abroad if you have been continuously incapable of work for the past six months. If you plan to go for an extended holiday, though, the Benefits Agency will look more closely at your case. It's wise to tell them well in advance, and in writing, about all the factors that make it reasonable and necessary for you to go abroad.

As explained on page 45, there's no formal right of appeal from a decision taken by the Secretary of State. But you can try to get the decision reversed – perhaps by getting a letter from your MP or from your doctor, social worker or health visitor.

People who went abroad before 7 March 1994

The rules explained above changed in 1994, so there are still quite a number of people who are receiving Incapacity Benefit who went abroad before that date and are covered by the earlier rules.

For them, benefit is payable for the whole of any temporary absence (not just 26 weeks), if either condition 1 or condition 2 has applied all the way through their absence. It's not necessary for the Secretary of State to give a certificate. There are also some special rules that will help people who go abroad with their sons or daughters who are serving members of the armed forces. They are counted as 'present' in the UK so long as they are with their children.

7 | Non-contributory benefits for people with disabilities

The benefits covered in this chapter are:

Severe Disablement Allowance (SDA);
Disability Living Allowance (DLA);
Attendance Allowance (AA);
Invalid Care Allowance (ICA).

These are non-contributory benefits, which means that you do not need to have made National Insurance contributions at any time in your working life in order to receive them. Instead, there are 'residence' and 'presence' conditions (explained on pp 64–65), and only very limited possibilities of claiming the benefit from abroad or taking it abroad.

Severe Disablement Allowance

This is a benefit for people who are unable to work because of long-term disability or sickness, and who have not paid enough contributions to get Incapacity Benefit. It's at a lower rate (roughly 60 per cent) than Incapacity Benefit, and has different conditions.

You must be under 65 when you first qualify and have been incapable of work for at least 28 weeks (there are special conditions for people who have been incapable of work since the age of 20 or earlier). For full details of the conditions for Severe Disablement Allowance, see *Your Rights* and Social Security claim pack SDA 1.

There are both 'residence' and 'presence' conditions for Severe Disablement Allowance. You have to be ordinarily resident in the UK, and to have been present for at least 26 of the last 52 weeks. What these terms mean is explained in the next section.

Immigration status

Since 5 February 1996, there has been an additional condition that your right to reside in the UK must not be subject to any limitations or conditions. So British and Irish nationals, Commonwealth nationals with right of abode (see explanation in Chapter 3) and any person who has indefinite right to stay without conditions can claim. This will include sponsored immigrants (even if they are classed as 'persons from abroad' for Income Support, as explained in Chapter 8).

Nationals of EEA countries, and their family members, may be entitled to claim, whether or not they have been employed or self-employed in the past.

There are special 'transitional' arrangements for people who were already entitled to the benefit at the time of the change. They can continue to receive benefit either until the next review of their claim or until the Home Office takes a further decision on their case. People with refugee status or with exceptional leave to remain may also be entitled. It may be worth checking any decision made to end your transitional protection, as it is not unknown for the Benefits Agency to make a mistake here.

'Residence' and 'ordinarily resident'

You are usually **resident** in the country where you have your home for the time being. It is possible to be resident in more than one country at a time, but this is unusual. You can remain resident in a place during a temporary absence, but it depends on the circumstances. Important factors in deciding the issue would be:

- where the rest of your family live;
- what sort of accommodation you have (whether you are staying in a hotel, or have rented an apartment, or bought a house, for instance);
- where your furniture and other personal possessions are kept.

If you move and are planning to settle at your new address, you are regarded as resident there from the first day.

Ordinarily resident takes you a step further. You are 'ordinarily resident' if there is a degree of continuity about your residence so that it can be described as settled. So if you live mostly in Great Britain but go elsewhere from time to time, you would still be regarded as ordinarily resident in Great Britain throughout the shorter periods elsewhere.

Residence in another EEA country, and in some of the countries with whom the UK has reciprocal agreements, may count towards UK residence.

If questions are raised by the Adjudication Officer, it is up to you to prove that you are or were 'resident' or 'ordinarily resident' at the relevant time.

> **Note** These definitions are not the same as the meaning of 'habitual residence', used in the law on means-tested benefits and covered in Chapter 8.

Presence

Presence simply means 'not absent'. You are present in the UK on any day you are in the country *throughout* the day (that is, from midnight to midnight). There are special arrangements to cover close relatives of serving members of the armed forces. If they go abroad, for instance with a son or daughter who is in the army, they continue to be counted as 'present' as long as they are living with them.

Going abroad with SDA

Severe Disablement Allowance is an 'exportable' benefit for EEA countries. However, as explained on page 60, the 'export' arrangements only come into play if you are employed or self-employed. Alternatively, the claim can be 'derived' if you are moving as part of the family of someone who is employed or self-employed. By the nature of things, most people getting Severe Disablement Allowance will not qualify independently as workers, so what matters is whether they can qualify as a family member. If this is not possible, they are covered only by any reciprocal agreement with the country in which they have been living – even if that is less favourable than the normal EEA rules. In other countries with reciprocal agreements, entitlement will depend on the precise terms.

If you are going to a country that is not in either of these categories, the rules on continuing to receive benefit are the same as for Incapacity Benefit (see p 61), and so quite restrictive.

Disability Living Allowance

Disability Living Allowance (DLA) is a benefit for people who become ill or disabled before the age of 65 (men and women). It is for disabled people who:

- need help with personal care, or need supervision, or need someone to watch over them (the 'care' component); *or*
- are unable to walk, or have great difficulty walking, or need someone with them when walking outdoors (the 'mobility' component); *or*
- need help with both of these.

It is payable at a number of different rates, depending on the severity of your needs.

For full details of the conditions for Disability Living Allowance, see *Your Rights* and Social Security leaflet DS704 and claim pack DLA 1. See also Age Concern's Factsheet 34, *Attendance Allowance and Disability Living Allowance.*

There are the same three conditions as for Severe Disablement Allowance (explained on pp 63–65) – that is:

- no limits on immigration status;
- ordinary residence;
- presence for at least 26 weeks in the past year.

Nationals of countries that have reciprocal agreements with Britain that allow periods of residence in another country to be treated as a period of residence in Britain are treated as satisfying the 'residence' condition. However, for the **presence** test (explained on p 65), periods of residence in another EEA country do not count.

There are special rules for claims from people who are certified as terminally ill, who are exempt from the rule that they must have been present in Great Britain for 26 weeks.

Going abroad with DLA

In practice, the rules mean that you must never spend more than six months abroad at a time and you should also keep a home in the UK, if you want to keep getting the benefit. The Government attempted to restrict payment of these benefits abroad, but found that under European law they were not able to do so.

Attendance Allowance

This is a benefit for people who become ill or disabled after the age of 65, covering the same 'care' needs as Disability Living Allowance does for those who become disabled at an earlier age. That is, that they need help with personal care, or need supervision, or need someone to watch over them. (There is no benefit to cover the 'mobility' needs of this group.) It can be paid at a higher or lower rate, depending on the extent of the need for care or supervision.

For full details of the conditions for Attendance Allowance, see *Your Rights* and Social Security leaflet DS702 and claim pack DS2. See also Age Concern's Factsheet 34, *Attendance Allowance and Disability Living Allowance.*

The rules on residence, presence and the right to reside are the same as for Disability Living Allowance (see above). So are the rules about taking the benefit abroad – that is, that you should not spend more than six months abroad at any time and you should also keep a home here. The transitional arrangements after the February 1996 changes are also the same (see p 64).

Invalid Care Allowance

Invalid Care Allowance (ICA) is a benefit for people who are unable to work full-time because they are caring for a severely disabled person for at least 35 hours a week. The person being cared for must be receiving:

- Attendance Allowance at the higher rate; or
- the care component of Disability Living Allowance at one of the higher rates; or
- Constant Attendance Allowance (for an industrial injury) at one of the higher rates.

For full details of the conditions for Invalid Care Allowance, see *Your Rights* and Social Security claim pack DS700, or information leaflet FB 31 *Caring for Someone?*. The Carers National Association produces information for carers. Their address is 20–25 Glasshouse Yard, London EC1A 4JS.

The rules on residence, presence and the right to reside are the same as for Disability Living Allowance (see p 66). The special 'transitional' arrangements after the February 1996 changes are also the same (p 64).

Because of the links with the other disability benefits, people may lose (or be unable to claim in future) Invalid Care Allowance *either* because of their own immigration status *or* because of the immigration status of the person they are caring for.

On the other hand, there are some people who do not claim Invalid Care Allowance when they are eligible, because they are better off if they claim Income Support instead. A person in this category who *loses* Income Support because of the 'habitual residence' rule (explained on pp 70–73) may still be able to claim Invalid Care Allowance under the different residence and presence rules for this benefit.

Going abroad with ICA

The rules are the same as for Disability Living Allowance and Attendance Allowance (with the same doubts over EEA countries), but in practice they would apply only if you were going abroad with the person for whom you were caring, except for very short breaks away. Essentially, the rules allow you to have four weeks' break in every six months, or for the disabled person to have four weeks in hospital at a time (12 weeks if they are under 16), without the carer losing benefit.

8 Income-related (means-tested) benefits

This chapter discusses benefits that older people may be able to claim, depending on their income and savings. It covers:

Income Support,
Housing Benefit and **Council Tax Benefit,**
each of which helps with regular weekly expenses.

The **Social Fund,** which provides lump sum payments and loans for exceptional expenses, is discussed in Chapter 9.

There have recently been major changes in the law on these benefits. The changes have the effect of restricting, or removing altogether, the rights of many people living in the UK, but who have come from abroad in the last few years, to claim these benefits.

Income Support

This benefit helps with weekly basic living expenses, by topping up your income to a level set by the Government. You do not need to have paid National Insurance contributions to qualify for Income Support, but your income and any savings and capital will be taken into account.

Income Support can be paid to home owners, to tenants, to people in other circumstances such as living with family and friends and indeed those who are homeless. It can qualify you for other benefits such as free dental treatment.

If you receive Income Support, you are also likely to qualify for Housing Benefit and/or Council Tax Benefit, which are based on similar rules (explained later in this chapter). For full details, see *Your Rights* and Social Security leaflet IS 20.

'Persons from abroad'

'Persons from abroad' are treated differently from other claimants for Income Support. In most cases, people classed as Persons from Abroad (PFAs) will be unable to claim Income Support, Housing Benefit or Council Tax Benefit. People affected by these rules include:

- those who fail the 'habitual residence' test;
- some 'sponsored immigrants';
- almost anyone who has a time limit on how long he or she may remain in the UK;
- certain people seeking asylum as refugees.

The rules about each of these groups are explained below.

Except for the 'habitual residence' rule or test, the PFA rules do not apply to UK citizens and nationals from the EEA (though in some cases benefit can be refused to EEA nationals, as explained below). For this purpose, Cyprus nationals do not count as 'persons from abroad'; neither do Maltese or Turkish nationals unless they have applied for the conditions under which they were allowed to enter the UK to be varied, nor people who have left Montserrat because of the volcanic eruption.

Habitual residence

In order to be able to claim Income Support, you must be able to show that you are 'habitually resident' in the UK, the Channel Islands or the Irish Republic (this is called the Common Travel Area or CTA). This applies to *all* claimants (but not their partners or dependants), including British citizens. But you are automatically treated as habitually resident in the UK and therefore exempt from the test if you are:

- An EEA citizen who is classified as a 'worker', or who has the right to reside in the UK under specified European legislation; this does not include the law, explained on page 20, that allows people to retire to another EEA state, however.
- Someone who has been accepted as a refugee or has been granted 'exceptional leave to remain' (but people who are still waiting for a decision come under different restrictions, explained on pp 75–76).

If you were entitled to Income Support on 31 July 1994, you will not have to satisfy the 'habitual residence' rule unless you make a new claim after that date – but simply filling in a new form after a change in circumstances should not count as a new claim.

People who make a claim for Income Support now are routinely asked whether they have entered the UK within the last five years; if they have, they will be given a further interview. If you are called for such an interview, take all the evidence with you that you can – it's better to have too many papers than too few.

When the rule was introduced in 1994, it was unclear for some time exactly what the definition of 'habitual residence' was, and there were a number of inconsistent decisions at local level. After a ruling by the Social Security Commissioners (the people at the second tier of appeals on Social Security issues), new guidance has been issued to Adjudication Officers, though there are still several legal challenges pending.

It is not possible, the Commissioners said, to give a complete definition of 'habitual residence'. Nor is it possible to list all the relevant facts – some that are relevant in one case may not be in another. But the facts in each case must be considered in a commonsense way. The Adjudication Officers' guidance says that:

- The most important factors for habitual residence are the length, continuity and general nature of *actual* residence, rather than future intentions.
- An 'appreciable period of time' together with a settled intention will be necessary to establish habitual residence. The relevant period is in the *past*, not a plan for the future.
- The length of the 'appreciable periods of time' will depend on the facts of each case.
- Accommodation must be 'viable' – that is, it must be possible to make and keep a home in the UK without help from public funds. Another Commissioner has said, though, that this is not a specific condition of being considered habitually resident, but simply one factor among all those to be taken into account.

On the period that would be counted as an 'appreciable period of time' CPAG's *National Welfare Benefits Handbook* (see p 109 for details) points out that two different Social Security Commissioners have stressed the need to consider the facts of each case. There is no minimum period, they say, but habitual residence cannot be acquired in a day.

Family law cases in instances of child abduction have shown that habitual residence can be acquired in a month. One Commissioner said that a citizen of the UK, of whatever ethnic origin, having lived abroad and without any ties overseas, could expect to become habitually resident after three months. The second Commissioner advised that Adjudication Officers should not rely on this example. There is a tendency for local offices to treat the three months as an unofficial minimum, but this is not right in terms of the law.

However, the same judgment said that someone who is already established as a habitual resident in this country, but happens to travel a lot, ought not to be treated in the same way so long as their absences are temporary (even if quite lengthy). If there is doubt in your case, you are entitled to the benefit of the doubt. If you are turned down at first, it is worth re-applying because establishing an 'appreciable period' is only a matter of time.

What about people who have come to the UK because they want to retire here? A later Commissioner's decision dealt specifically with this. A UK national who had worked abroad and who intended to settle here on his retirement could count towards the 'appreciable periods of time' the periods when he had, for example, searched for a property in which to live on his return.

In 1995/6, over 6000 British citizens returning from abroad failed the 'habitual residence' test, along with around the same number from EEA countries and 7000 from elsewhere. The European Commission, having first accepted that the test did not conflict with European law, said in the summer of 1996 that it was reconsidering the issue. It has been referred to a 'high-level panel' considering the free movement of people within the European Union. It is to be hoped that, now the law has been clarified, fewer people who have established links with the UK will be denied Income Support under this test.

If you are turned down by the Adjudication Officer under this rule, it is usually worth appealing, because the Social Security Appeal Tribunal may take a different view. Ask for the hearing of your appeal to be speeded up if you are suffering hardship.

Even if you fail in your first claim, try again later – especially if there is a change in your circumstances, or simply after what seems like enough time has passed. Making repeated claims will highlight your determination to remain in the UK.

Sponsored immigrants

As explained in Chapter 3, many people who have come to the UK from other countries have been 'sponsored', generally by close relatives. The rules on benefits for people being sponsored also changed in February 1996. The change applies only to people whose sponsors signed a legal undertaking to maintain and accommodate them.

When an undertaking *has* been signed, a sponsored immigrant will not be entitled to Income Support for the first five years living in the UK unless:

- their sponsor dies; or
- they acquire British citizenship.

If the sponsor dies, the sponsored person will be able to claim Income Support but only at a special lower 'Urgent Cases' rate – 90 per cent of the personal rate, plus any premiums he or she may be entitled to – until the end of five years from the date of entry or from the date of the undertaking, whichever is later.

There is special 'transitional' protection for people already receiving Income Support at the time the law changed. They are unaffected.

> **Gloria** came to the UK in November 1993 as a sponsored immigrant, with indefinite leave to remain. She claimed Income Support in February 1994, and was able to carry on receiving it when the law changed in February 1996. In November 1997 she goes abroad for an extended holiday. When she returns, she should still be entitled to full Income Support; the Benefits Agency might disagree, though, so an appeal may be needed.

Recovering money from a sponsor

For people who have been receiving Income Support so far, if there was a mandatory undertaking (that is, the sponsor guaranteed that they would provide maintenance and accommodation), the Benefits Agency have the power to recover from the sponsor the amount of Income Support paid. They are unlikely to use their power, however, if the sponsor cannot afford to pay.

However, if the undertaking was given many years ago, before 23 May 1980, the Benefits Agency do not have the power to recover the money.

Asylum seekers

Chapter 3 explained that there is a right under UN conventions and international law to claim asylum (refugee status) in another country. But since February 1996, Britain has imposed tight restrictions on Social Security claims by people in this position. There have been several court challenges to the new arrangements, and it is possible that the British Government may yet have to change these rules to meet European requirements.

Until February 1996, people claiming asylum were classified as 'persons from abroad' (PFAs), and did not have the right to claim the full level of Income Support. But they *could* have had entitlement to a very basic level, under the rules covering Urgent Cases Payments (UCPs), and did not have to pass the 'habitual residence test' (explained on pp 70–73).

With the change in the rules, what matters is the date when you arrived, the point at which you made the claim for asylum and the dates the Home Office takes decisions about it. In general, you will now be refused any help unless you apply for asylum 'on arrival' in the UK. That has been interpreted as meaning at immigration control, but this is debatable. It will be worth appealing in cases of doubt.

If you have applied at the right point and are granted Income Support, but your asylum application is then turned down, payment of Income Support will then stop.

There is some protection for people who had already claimed benefit before the change. In addition, because of successful court challenges about the Government's original regulations, those who arrived between 5 February and 25 July 1996 (when the Government was forced to bring in emergency legislation) are in a special position.

In essence, people who claimed asylum between February and July 1996 *can* have benefit, under the old rules. But the DSS are making no effort to find those who were refused Income Support earlier, for the period up to 25 July 1996. Anyone in this position (or with a friend or relative in this position) should be advised to contact the Refugee

Council as soon as possible, or a local organisation or solicitor if there is one specialising in this area.

Applying on arrival

You may be able to qualify for Income Support (at the Urgent Cases rate explained above) while waiting for a decision from the Home Office, if you apply for asylum 'on arrival' in Great Britain. These payments are available, though, only if you have no other income or capital. The rule about 'on arrival' is being interpreted by the DSS to mean immediately and at the port or airport of entry. For example:

> **Radovan** arrives in Heathrow with a visa as a visitor. He goes through passport control at Heathrow, is granted leave to enter, and gets an internal flight to Glasgow. At Glasgow he claims asylum. According to the DSS, there is no entitlement to Urgent Cases Payments because the application was not made when the person from abroad first arrived in the UK.

If a person applied for asylum 'on arrival' in the UK, although not immediately on entry to an Immigration Officer, it is possible to challenge the interpretation of the rules by the DSS and appeal against the refusal. Ask for advice (see list of possible sources of help on pp 117–119) first.

A person will not qualify for Urgent Cases Payments if they make an application for asylum on 're-entry' to the UK. So, if someone were to arrive and find lodging, and then go to another country to collect their family, they would not be able to make a claim under this rule.

> **Note** For this purpose, the Channel Islands, Isle of Man and Republic of Ireland are regarded differently. They are not part of Great Britain but are in the 'Common Travel Area'. So someone who goes first, say, to Jersey and then applies for asylum as soon as he or she gets off the ferry on the UK mainland has not applied from 'outside the Common Travel Area' and will not qualify under this rule. The application must be made on arrival.

Applying because of an upheaval

You *can* qualify for Income Support as an asylum seeker if, while you are in Great Britain, the Secretary of State has declared the conditions of your country of origin and nationality to be such that you could not normally be returned to it, *and* you then make the application. The application for asylum must be made within three months after the date the declaration is made. The intention is that, if there is a major political upheaval in a country, the Government could declare that the country is 'subject to such a fundamental change in circumstances' that Income Support will be paid in these cases. So far, only former Zaire is in this category. Payment will be at the Urgent Cases rate only.

In addition, to apply while in the UK you must have the nationality of the country from which you are seeking asylum – for example, you must be a Zairean if you are seeking asylum so that you need not go back to Zaire. So if you are stateless, or have been living in a country without holding its nationality, you will not qualify under this rule.

When a decision is taken on your case

It can take some time for a decision to be taken on an asylum claim. Once a decision is made on the individual's case:

- if refugee status or Exceptional Leave to Remain is granted, he or she can claim Income Support under the normal rules;
- if asylum is refused, Income Support stops immediately, even if the individual appeals.

However, in cases where the original refusal decision was taken before 5 February 1996, Income Support will continue until the appeal is heard.

Documents for asylum seekers

There can be problems in providing evidence of your identity and status, if you have come to the UK without the usual travel and identity documents, or with false ones.

If you apply at the port of entry (as explained on p 75), you should be issued with a Standard Acknowledgement Letter (SAL1), and a form IS96 confirming that you have been granted temporary admission. These documents should be accepted by the Benefits Agency as sufficient for making a claim. If you have only form IS96 and not SAL1, you can still claim Income Support but you may encounter difficulties at the local Benefits Agency. However, they should not refuse you payment simply because you do not have the SAL1.

If you apply for asylum after coming to the UK, you will be given a GEN32 form calling you for interview, and later a second Standard Acknowledgement Letter (SAL2). Again, these should be accepted as sufficient evidence of identity by the Benefits Agency, but do not mean that you qualify for Income Support.

If for some reason you have none of these things, the Benefits Agency will probably phone the Home Office to confirm your status. They should be willing to interview you to establish your identity, and should take account of relevant correspondence about your application for asylum, perhaps from a lawyer or an advice agency.

Recourse to public funds

As explained in Chapter 3, many people who are admitted to the UK are given only limited leave to remain, on condition that they do not have 'recourse to public funds'. Income Support (and the other benefits covered in this chapter) are 'public funds' for this purpose and so anyone still subject to this condition will not be able to get benefit unless they are covered by the provision for Urgent Cases Payments explained above.

The only other exception is people who depend on funds from abroad and whose source of funding has stopped temporarily. They can obtain an Urgent Cases Payment for a short time, up to 42 days, so long as there is a 'reasonable expectation' that the flow of funds will resume.

In some cases, one partner in a couple will be able to claim Income Support while the other is a 'person from abroad' and cannot do so. In that case, if the claimant is not receiving any Income Support for his or her partner, this is not breaking the 'public funds' restriction. But you should always get advice before claiming Income Support if your spouse or fiancé(e) is applying for entry clearance – it could be taken as an indication that you are not able to maintain them, and so could jeopardise their application.

Other 'persons from abroad'

People classed by the Home Office as illegal entrants or overstayers, or subject to a deportation order, are not eligible for Income Support.

> **Note** Anyone in this position should seek advice before they even approach the Benefits Agency.

If you are waiting for a decision on your immigration status, or have made an appeal against a decision, you too may not claim Income Support. An exception is if you are appealing against an asylum decision and you are covered by the transitional arrangements (see p 74).

Nationals of other EEA countries can be sent a letter by the Home Office telling them that they are no longer lawfully resident in the UK and that they are required to leave (though there's some doubt about whether this is legal under European law). This rule could be used against a pensioner, for instance, who was in the UK under the rights given in the 1992 Directive (see p 20), which requires them to be self-supporting. Although Income Support, Housing Benefit and Council Tax Benefit will stop in these circumstances, people are unlikely to be deported as a result of making a claim.

What to do if you are refused benefit

You *might* be able to get a crisis loan under the Social Fund (see Chapter 9) if you are refused benefit. But as these loans are given only if you will be able to repay them, having no prospect of future income may prevent your receiving one.

In some (rare) cases it may be possible to apply for an *ex-gratia* or extra-statutory payment (that is, a special payment altogether outside the rules) if someone has no income. The best way to do this will be to approach your MP for help.

Another possibility is to approach the Social Services Department of the local council. Asylum seekers have no right to help under the normal laws requiring local authorities to help homeless people (under the 1996 Housing Act). However, assistance might be available for a vulnerable older person under the Community Care legislation which covers people who are in need of care because of their mental or physical condition. You may want to take it up with a councillor as well as with the officers.

In practice, it seems as if most of the people who have been refused benefit, or had it cut off as a result of the changes in the law, are finding help from local authority social services under the 1948 National Assistance Act, within their communities, from churches and voluntary organisations, and from their families or extended families who are often suffering great strain in providing this help. There have also been press reports that organisations are going to have to set up 'tent villages' to cope with the destitute people coming to them. The Refugee Council have already set up a hostel for this purpose.

People who are able to claim Income Support

If you are not excluded in one of the ways listed above, you may receive Income Support if:

- your savings are £8000 or less (or £16,000 if you live in a residential or nursing home);
- you have a low income;
- you are not working more than 16 hours a week, and your partner is not working more than 24 hours a week.

A 'partner' is your husband or wife, or someone of the opposite sex whom you live with as though you were married. So it is quite possible for someone to be disallowed a retirement pension as a married woman because the marriage is not recognised as valid in the UK (see p 55) but still to be treated as part of a couple when she claims Income Support.

If you are part of a heterosexual couple, one person applies for Income Support for both him- or herself and the partner. It's for you to choose whether the man or the woman claims. If you live with someone else such as a friend or relative, you can both apply for Income Support separately.

For more information on how Income Support is worked out, look in *Your Rights*, or in CPAG's *National Welfare Benefits Handbook* if you want all the legal details. The rest of this section covers only areas that may raise particular problems for people from ethnic minorities.

If your partner is abroad

If your partner is abroad but intends to come to the UK, and you have lived together as a couple abroad, you may not be entitled to Income Support. This is because you are treated as being members of the same household (even though you might be separated by thousands of miles), so the income and savings of both partners will be added together.

But if your partner is abroad permanently, you can claim Income Support as a single person.

Savings and property abroad

As explained above, one of the conditions for claiming Income Support is that the individual or couple has savings of £8000 or less (£16,000 if you live in a residential or nursing home). 'Savings' here means capital, savings, investments and property.

The value of the house you own and live in is normally ignored for this purpose. However, if you have other property elsewhere, such as land or a house in your country of origin, or investments in a bank abroad, this *will* be taken into account. If there are no currency exchange controls or other prohibitions that would stop you transferring your capital to this country, the assets are valued at their current market value in that country. There could be some delays in getting a proper valuation of your assets; if so, you may be able to get an 'interim payment' of Income Support (or a 'payment on account' of Housing Benefit or Council Tax Benefit).

In deciding what value to put on the property, you are allowed to deduct 10 per cent of the market value for the cost of making the sale, and also the value of any mortgage or other debt secured on the property. The 'market value' is the amount that a willing buyer would give to a willing seller – so in some cases it may be heavily reduced or even nothing at all.

If you would not be allowed to transfer the full value of your capital to the UK, you are treated as having capital of the amount that a willing buyer in this country would give for those assets – which, again, might be very different from their actual value. Ask for advice if you think these rules are being applied unfairly in your case.

There are some special rules about what happens while you are trying to sell a home, or when you have received the capital but plan to use it for another home, and in some other special circumstances. Get advice if you think one of these rules could apply to you.

Housing Benefit and Council Tax Benefit

Housing Benefit provides help with rent and with some service charges (and with general rates in Northern Ireland). **Council Tax Benefit** provides help with paying Council Tax. You may get these benefits if you have a low income and your savings are no more than £16,000. Both these benefits are administered by the local council, and you should enquire there if you think you may be eligible.

For more information on how Housing Benefit and Council Tax Benefit are worked out, look in *Your Rights*, or in CPAG's *National Welfare Benefits Handbook* if you want all the legal details. The rest of this section covers only areas that may raise particular problems for people from ethnic minorities.

The same rules on 'persons from abroad' and 'habitual residence' apply as for Income Support, as explained above. So if you are not eligible for Income Support you will generally not be eligible for Housing Benefit or Council Tax Benefit either. However, some local authorities are imposing the habitual residence test only on people who have been here less than two years (rather than five as for Income Support), so it may be possible to qualify for Housing Benefit and/or Council Tax Benefit even when not getting Income Support.

There is very likely to be liaison between local authorities and the Immigration and Nationality Department to check claimants' immigration status. You should be told if the council are intending to do this, but many Housing Benefit application forms now have a standard section which, when you sign the form, grants the council permission to check. There is also liaison with the Benefits Agency if you are claiming Income Support as well, and information you give to one department could be passed to another.

You may be interviewed to check whether you are entitled to claim, and you will be asked to produce proof of your identity and immigration status – usually a passport.

If you are unsure how a claim for Housing Benefit and/or Council Tax Benefit might affect your right (or your partner's right) to remain in the UK, get *independent advice* about this before putting in a claim. If you find out later that you can claim without any problems, ask for your benefit to be backdated on the grounds that you have 'good cause' for a late claim.

There are various other ways in which a Council Tax bill can be reduced, which are summarised in *Your Rights*. These include special exemptions for some properties, and discounts if a person lives alone or with someone who is not counted for this purpose. If you are not eligible to claim Council Tax Benefit, check whether any of these discounts could help you instead.

The rules on capital and income are broadly the same as for Income Support, with a few variations, so the same problems with property or income abroad can arise.

If you are living with your family

If you are living with a landlord who is a close relative, you will be able to claim Housing Benefit if you live separately in self-contained accommodation. However, you cannot claim if you are part of the same household or if it is not a 'commercial arrangement'. Get advice if you are unsure about the position.

If either or both of you goes abroad

If one person in a couple goes abroad *temporarily*, and intends to return within 52 weeks, you will continue to be treated as a couple for Housing Benefit purposes. But if one of a couple leaves *permanently*, you will be treated as a single person and should claim immediately on that basis.

If a single person, or both of a couple, goes abroad temporarily, Housing Benefit will, in most cases, continue to be paid for only 13 weeks. However, there are some limited cases where it can carry on for 52 weeks. The relevant ones are:

- you are undertaking medically approved treatment or convalescence in the UK or abroad; or
- you are providing, or receiving, medically approved care in the UK or abroad.

But to be eligible for Housing Benefit, of course, you must retain responsibility for payments on your home. If you give up your tenancy, or sub-let to someone else, you must tell the local council, who will adjust or stop your benefit.

9 | The Social Fund

The Social Fund provides lump sum payments to people with low incomes, in order to meet exceptional expenses. You may be able to get help from the 'discretionary' Social Fund, in the form of Community Care Grants, or Budgeting or Crisis Loans. You may also be able to get help from the 'regulated' Social Fund for the cost of funerals, and cold weather payments.

This chapter considers:

community care grants;
crisis loans; and
funeral payments.

For more details about the Social Fund, see *Your Rights* and Social Security leaflet SFL 2 or detailed guide SB 16.

Community care grants

These are available to people receiving Income Support, and do not have to be repaid. The budget for each local DSS office is very limited, but it could be worth applying; for example, for refugees and asylum seekers who are having to set up home from scratch after having lived in a hostel for a while. Even if you are not sure whether you will get help, you have nothing to lose by applying.

Alternatively, such people may be offered **budgeting loans** to meet their needs. Although these may help, the disadvantage is that they will have to be paid back out of an already low income. So it will be worth pressing for a grant rather than a loan.

Crisis loans

These are interest-free loans, available to anyone (not just people on Income Support, as for other parts of the 'discretionary' Social Fund) who needs money urgently in an emergency, or who has been involved in a disaster such as fire or flood. The Social Fund Officer will take into account all the family's savings and income that are available to you. You may be able to get a loan, provided this is the only way of preventing serious risk to your health or safety, or that of a member of your family.

In theory, these loans should be available to people who may not receive Income Support because of one of the rules explained in Chapter 8. However, the loans will be awarded only if the officer thinks you will be able to repay them. So if you have no prospect of any income in the future, you will probably not receive one.

People from abroad who, because of their immigration status, would not be entitled to Income Support at either the normal rate or the Urgent Cases rate, can claim a crisis loan only for expenses arising because of a disaster. Many asylum seekers are now in this position, as most are no longer entitled to Income Support, as explained in Chapter 8. So to get a crisis loan, they would have to show that their situation constitutes a disaster and that they are likely to be able to repay the loan.

People from abroad who *are* entitled to Income Support can claim a crisis loan in the normal way. Social Fund Officers are advised to give particular attention to the clothing needs of refugees and asylum seekers. But asylum seekers should also be encouraged and supported in applying for community care grants, as explained above.

> **Note** If you are an overstayer, subject to a deportation order, or an illegal entrant, you should not apply for a crisis loan before getting advice about regularising your status here.

Funeral costs

If you are responsible for the cost of a funeral for your partner or a close relative or close friend, you may be able to get help from the Social

Fund if you are already claiming a means-tested benefit. 'Partner' means the person you were married to, or living with as their husband or wife. 'Close relative' is defined very narrowly, so many people in extended families, who might think of themselves as close, will not qualify. It means:

- parent, parent-in-law, or step-parent;
- son, son-in-law, stepson or stepson-in-law;
- daughter, daughter-in-law, stepdaughter, stepdaughter-in-law;
- brother or brother-in-law;
- sister or sister-in-law.

Uncles, aunts and cousins do not count, but might be able to show that they were a 'close friend'. When there is more than one close relative, the nature and extent of contact that each one had with the deceased person will be considered.

If there is a close relative who had more contact with the person who has died than you do, or if there is another person equally close who is not on a means-tested benefit or has more savings than you, they will be expected to take responsibility for the funeral instead of you.

Up to £500 can be paid to meet the costs of arranging the funeral, including such things as transport and the price of the coffin. Some other expenses can be paid, including:

- up to £75 for additional costs because of the requirements of the religious faith of the person who has died; and
- the reasonable cost of one return journey in the UK to allow you to attend or arrange the funeral (including overnight expenses if needed).

The expenses of a funeral abroad, or of bringing a body back to the UK from abroad, will not be covered. One exception to this, as a result of a recent European Court case, is that funerals in other member states of the European Union should be covered (there will probably be a change in the Regulations at some point to deal with this). However, the court did say that there was nothing to prevent the UK from limiting the grant to the normal cost of a funeral in the UK.

Any savings of more than £1000 will be taken into account (or £500 if you are aged under 60). So if you have £1300, you would be expected to pay £300 towards the funeral, and then get help with the rest up to the maximum limit. Money due from an insurance policy or pension scheme, or any other payment due on the death, is also taken into account.

If the person who has died has left money or property, the DSS will usually reclaim the funeral payment from these before anything is paid out to the heirs. The rules about capital or property abroad are the same as for Income Support (see Chapter 8).

10 Health and social care

Primary health care

Anyone, regardless of their immigration status or length of residence, is able to register with a General Practitioner (GP) as an NHS patient, for the basic health care – such as dealing with minor illnesses and accidents for which you do not need to go to hospital. However, GPs can refuse to take a particular patient onto their books, if they feel that the person will be difficult to deal with or they are too busy. It may be necessary at times to try several GPs. Ultimately, the local Family Practitioner Committee can allocate people to a GP's practice if they have been unable to find one themselves.

Hospital charges

Most of the treatment given under the National Health Service is free to people living in the UK. But people visiting this country for short stays can be asked to pay various charges for most NHS hospital services. These will not apply if you have been living in the UK for at least the previous 12 months, or if you have come with the intention of remaining permanently but are waiting for the Home Office to agree to an application for settlement. Asylum seekers are also exempt from NHS charges.

For more information, see *The Patients' Guide: National Health Service hospital charges for overseas visitors*, published by NHS Management Executive. This should be available from the Patient Affairs Department of an NHS hospital.

There are some exemptions from the charges for overseas visitors, including treatment in accident and emergency (casualty) departments, compulsory psychiatric treatment, and diagnosis and treatment of certain communicable diseases.

UK state pensioners living overseas do not have to pay for certain emergency treatment, if the need arises while they are in the UK. War disablement pensioners and war widows are also exempt. Citizens of the EU need not pay charges, and the UK has reciprocal medical agreements with certain other countries. However, these agreements vary, and some only cover treatment for conditions that have arisen during the visit. You should check with your own consulate for details.

Anyone who comes to a UK hospital for the first time should be asked up to three brief questions, to decide whether they are eligible for free treatment. If they answer yes to either of the first two questions, they have shown they are entitled to free treatment. The questions are:

- Have you or your husband or wife been living in the UK for the past 12 months?
- Are you or your husband or wife going to live in the UK permanently?
- On what date did you or your husband or wife arrive in the UK?

Hospital administrators should not ask to see passports at this stage, unless they have reason to believe they have not been told the truth. (In fact, they often do ask.)

If the patient has answered 'no' to the first two questions, they will be asked further questions (called Stage 2 questioning). There is a *Manual of Guidance for Health Service Charges*, which gives complicated flow charts for administrators to use. The instructions are that passports should be asked for only at this stage, and then only to check if people are citizens of a country with which there is a reciprocal agreement.

If charges are made, they are the normal private rates for treatment, without any extra consultants' fees. The Department of Health publishes a list of the fees for particular treatments, drugs and operations as well as 'boarding' fees (the cost of food and 'hotel' services). They vary according to the type of hospital.

There is no power to charge anyone except the patient for medical treatment. So hospitals have no authority to ask the relatives or friends of a visitor to pay or to guarantee payments for medical treatment, though they may try to obtain such guarantees in practice.

Charges for other health costs

There are some items for which most people have to pay some or all of the cost. These include dental care, eye tests and glasses. The details of what is available are explained in *Your Rights*.

People receiving Income Support automatically get help with these costs by showing their order book or a letter from the Benefits Agency. However, if you have not been able to get Income Support, but have less than £8000 savings, you can apply for 'low income entitlement'. Get form AG1/HC1 from your local Benefits Agency office, or from a hospital. Some dentists, opticians and GP surgeries also have them.

If you qualify for help with these costs, you will be sent a certificate lasting for six months. Certificate AG2/HC2 entitles you to the same amount of help as people receiving Income Support. If your income is a little higher, you may get certificate AG3/HC3, which entitles you to more limited help. There is also some help, on the same basis, with the cost of travel to hospital.

If you cannot receive Income Support because you are a 'person from abroad', as explained in Chapter 8, you should apply for help with these costs when needed.

Prescriptions

Prescriptions are free to anyone over 60. For someone younger than that, they are free to anyone on Income Support or there is the 'low income' test as explained above. Again, you can apply even if you are not eligible for Income Support.

Health costs abroad

In general, if you go to another country you are covered by their rules on paying for health costs. In some cases, such as the USA, these can be enormous, especially if a hospital stay is involved, and it is essential to take out adequate insurance before you go. Some reciprocal agreements cover health costs, but by no means all.

As so often, though, the situation in the EEA is different. If you receive a state pension, widow's benefit or incapacity benefit and you move to another EEA country, you and dependent members of your family will generally be entitled to the health services of the sickness insurance scheme of that country. But you must obtain DSS form E111 (from your local Benefits Agency) before you leave the UK.

UK nationals officially resident in another EEA country will have the same entitlement to medical and health care treatment as a national in the country they are living in. Check before you move what services exist, however, as these will not be the same as in the UK. Longer term health needs, such as community care services and hospices, may not exist.

There will be different entitlements for people who have not yet reached the state retirement age of the country they are moving to. You might, for instance, be required to pay for medical care or prescriptions.

As explained above, if you come back to the UK for a short visit you will be asked to pay hospital charges.

For more information, see leaflet T5 *Health Advice for Travellers*, available from the Benefits Agency.

Coming to the UK for private medical treatment

People who are ill can come to the UK as 'medical visitors', under special rules. To do this, you have to meet all the normal requirements explained in Chapter 3, and *also* show that:

- the course of medical treatment is of limited duration and you intend to leave at the end of it; and
- you have evidence of the medical condition requiring consultation or treatment in the UK, arrangements for private medical treatment, the estimated costs and timescale, and the funds available for it. You may be asked for an undertaking to pay.

If the disease is infectious, the Medical Inspector at the port of arrival has to be satisfied that there is no danger to public health. The rules do not say anything about whether the treatment is available in the person's home country, but this is certainly something that the Immigration Officers would take into account.

Medical visitors can be admitted for up to six months initially, but their stay can be extended if necessary.

Community care and Social Services help

This section deals with:

paying for community care or other help; and
finding services that are acceptable.

However, this book does not cover in detail questions of help for older people in residential care or to stay in their own homes. See pages 121–123 for details of Age Concern publications that do this.

Paying for care

If you want to go into a residential or nursing home and need help to pay the fees, you will have to be assessed by the local authority, to measure your care needs. If after this the local authority agree to arrange a place for you in a private or voluntary residential home, they will be responsible for paying the full fee to the home and assessing your income and savings to decide how much you should pay towards this.

People who are eligible for Income Support, and have less than £16,000 capital, may be able to receive help from the local authority. They will encourage you to claim any Income Support that you are entitled to, and then assess how much you should contribute towards the fees. The calculations are done under the normal rules, but there is an extra 'Residential Allowance' of £62 a week for homes in Greater London or £56 a week elsewhere (1997/8). The local authority will then take account of your income, plus an assumed ('tariff') income from savings, in deciding how much you must pay to them for the fees.

On the other hand, if you go into a home run by the local authority, you cannot claim the ordinary Income Support or Residential Allowance. Instead, if your capital is less than £16,000, you may be able to claim enough Income Support to give you the ordinary level of basic pension. From this, you would pay the local authority £48.35 a week (1997/8 rates), and keep £14.10 as an allowance for personal expenses.

If you are not eligible for Income Support because of one of the rules about 'persons from abroad' (explained in Chapter 8), you can still apply for help from the local authority. The local authority may be reluctant to help you because they will have to pay more for the cost of your care, as they can only charge you against any income you have, which may be very little or nothing. However, in principle, you should be offered the care you need even if you cannot pay anything towards it. If you have problems in getting help from the local authority in these circumstances, get advice.

If you have capital or property abroad

The value of an owner-occupied home will usually be taken into account in assessing what contribution you should pay towards your care, unless you have a partner or an elderly or disabled relative still living there. Property or capital abroad will be taken into account, but the rules on this largely follow those explained on page 80.

An important difference, though, is that, if your property is up for sale, its value is taken into account immediately (rather than after 26 weeks). The capital is counted immediately as part of the assessment. The local authority may then cover your costs while the sale is going through, but then ask for full repayment once the capital is available.

Finding acceptable services

According to Herman Ouseley of the Commission for Racial Equality;

> 'it is often argued that ethnic minority older people are looked after by their families or all ethnic minority older people return 'home' in old age, but there is little hard evidence to confirm that view as being accurate.'

According to specialist charity Counsel and Care, there is an urgent need to make care services more sensitive to the requirements of older people from ethnic minorities (ethnic elders). They point out that there is a considerable lack of knowledge among ethnic elders of what is available. Many people, they say, are reluctant even to consider going into residential care because of fears that they will not be able to follow their culture or dietary requirements. So a first step in seeking residential care – or indeed help in their own home (domiciliary help) – must be to ensure that people's special needs can be provided for.

Important issues are: the opportunity to follow one's own religion and to have a religious leader available to call at the home; provision of professional interpreting services where necessary and the employment of bilingual staff; creating links with local music, dance or drama groups that draw on traditions other than the Christian one – so that more than just the annual carol service is available – and the provision of detailed information about what is on offer.

Counsel and Care have translated about 20 of their factsheets on residential care issues into eight other languages. But they stress that a number of older people will not be able to read or write either in English or in their own language, and so efforts at communication ought to include the spoken word – local radio programmes, for instance – as well as the written.

11 War pensions

The War Pensions scheme is separate from the Social Security system, although it is administered by the Department of Social Security. It is mainly intended to provide pensions for disablements that are due to, or made worse by, service in the armed forces between August 1914 and September 1921, or after September 1939. Some other groups of people are also eligible. The coverage is for disablement attributed to:

- or aggravated by, service in HM Armed Forces (including the Ulster Defence Regiment, Home Guard, and Nursing and Auxiliary Services);
- certain injuries due to wartime services in the Naval Auxiliary Services, coastguard, or merchant navy;
- or aggravated by, service in the Polish Forces under British Command in World War II, or the Polish Resettlement Forces;
- certain injuries suffered by Civil Defence Volunteers or civilians during World War II.

There is a basic war disablement pension (which varies according to your rank during the war and with the level of your disability) and various supplementary allowances. For a relatively minor disability, a lump sum 'gratuity' can be paid instead of a pension.

There's no time limit for making a claim, but any award is normally paid only from the date of your claim. If it is over seven years since the incident that caused your disablement, or since you left the forces, it is up to you to prove your claim, and this is likely to be more difficult the longer you have waited. However, there are still people making claims now for injuries caused in World War II (and later conflicts).

Because the rules for claiming a war pension are very different from those for claiming any other sort of pension, people who have been unable to receive other state benefits could find, if they had war service and were wounded, that they do have some potential benefit. The local War Pensioners' Welfare Office (address in the local phone book) will help with making claims, or check whether there are any extra allowances that could be claimed by someone who is already a war pensioner. It can also give advice on any other problem, and keeps closely in touch with the DSS, local authorities and voluntary organisations.

Claiming from abroad or going abroad

War pensions can be paid overseas, whether you are there temporarily or permanently. The War Pensions Agency ask you to notify them if you will be abroad for more than three months. There are also special arrangements for paying the cost of medical treatment for the accepted war disability while abroad. It is important to get this arranged before treatment is given, otherwise it is difficult to get the money back. The War Pensions Agency leaflet 6 explains the details.

There is an extensive network of Overseas Pensions Agents and Departments of Veterans' Affairs (listed in the War Pensions Agency leaflet 3), mainly based in embassies and consulates. They provide a service to help war pensioners and war widows/widowers to get help and advice on any sort of problem, as well as on war pensions themselves.

For information on war pensions, call the War Pensions Helpline on 01253 858858, or write to the War Pensions Agency, Norcross, Blackpool FY5 3WP, or the local War Pensioners' Welfare Office. Look also at WPA leaflet 1, *Notes about War Pensions and Allowances*; leaflet 3, *Notes for people getting a war pension (overseas)*; and leaflet 6, *Notes for war pensioners and war widows going abroad*.

APPENDIX 1
Abbreviations and glossary

Abbreviations

AA	Attendance Allowance
AO	Adjudication Officer
BA	Benefits Agency
BDTC	British Dependent Territories Citizen
BNO	British National (Overseas)
BOC	British Overseas Citizen
BPP	British protected person
CPAG	Child Poverty Action Group
CTA	Common Travel Area
CTB	Council Tax Benefit
CUKC	Citizen of the United Kingdom and Colonies
DLA	Disability Living Allowance
DSS	Department of Social Security
EEA	European Economic Area
EU	European Union
GP	general practitioner
HB	Housing Benefit
ICA	Invalid Care Allowance
ICB	Incapacity Benefit
IO	Immigration Officer
IS	Income Support

JCWI	Joint Council for the Welfare of Immigrants
MP	Member of Parliament
NHS	National Health Service
NI	National Insurance
PFA	person from abroad
POD	Pensions and Overseas Pensions Directorate (part of the DSS)
REC	Racial Equality Council
SDA	Severe Disablement Allowance
SERPS	State Earnings Related Pension Scheme
SSAT	Social Security Appeal Tribunal
UCP	Urgent Cases Payment
UN	United Nations

Glossary

Aggregation This is a rule that applies when you claim certain Social Security benefits for the first time in a EEA country. It is highly complicated, but means basically that you receive benefit only from the last country where you were insured, and involves treating periods of insurance or residence in other countries as though they were periods in the country where you were last insured. It is explained further on page 49.

Alien Broadly speaking, anyone who is not a Commonwealth citizen or a citizen of one of the countries of the European Economic Area (EEA). British citizens come in two groups, as explained below. The first group can pass on British citizenship automatically to their children born outside the UK, and the second cannot.

British citizens by descent are people who were born outside the UK, but became British automatically at birth because a parent or grandparent was born in the UK. For those born before 1 January 1983, this has to be the father (or in some cases the father's father); for those born after that date, it can be mother or father.

British citizens otherwise than by descent are people who acquired their citizenship by being born in the UK, or by being naturalised or registered in the UK, and also people who had a connection to a British colony or ex-colony and were settled in the UK for at least five years before 1983.

British nationals All British *citizens* are British nationals, but there are some other people who are British *nationals* without being citizens, and so don't have the 'right of abode' (explained below) in the UK. These are people who are British Overseas citizens, British Dependent Territories citizens, British Protected Persons and British Nationals (Overseas). Most British subjects are not citizens either, except for some very small groups, as explained on page 7.

British National (Overseas) This special status was created for British Dependent Territory citizens from Hong Kong to enable them to keep this British nationality status when Hong Kong reverted to China in 1997.

British Overseas citizen Someone who was born in a place that used to be a British colony, but who did not qualify for citizenship under the law of the new independent country. He or she therefore retained British nationality.

British Protected Person Someone from a country that used to be a British protectorate, protected state or trust territory rather than a colony, but who did not gain the citizenship of the new independent territory or any other country.

British subject Someone from a country that used to be a British colony, who never became a citizen of the UK and colonies under the British Nationality Act 1948, and who did not acquire citizenship of the new independent country or of any other country.

Certificate of identity Some people, including many from Hong Kong, have brown British travel documents called certificates of identity, but they are not any kind of British nationals. In effect they are stateless and have no special rights.

Commonwealth citizen All British nationals, except British Protected Persons, are Commonwealth citizens. So are citizens of the countries that gained independence within the Commonwealth. A complete list of these is given in the *Immigration and Nationality Law Handbook* (see also pp 102–103).

Condition of entry There are conditions laid down by the Home Office before they will allow you to enter the UK. Usually these will be stamped or written in your passport (called 'endorsing' the passport) by Immigration Officers when you arrive, although sometimes in the past this was not done.

Domicile This means the country to which people feel they belong and in which they intend to spend the rest of their life. Normally people are considered to have a 'domicile of origin', usually the country in which they were born and grew up. This can be changed only by a conscious decision to settle and stay in another country and thus acquire a 'domicile of choice'. People's immigration status has no direct connection with their domicile.

Entry clearance relates to the process that someone who is a visa national (which see) has to go through in advance, before travelling to the UK. They must apply to have their passport endorsed with a UK visa for the purpose for which they seek entry. This is done at a UK High Commission, Embassy or Consulate. However, someone with entry clearance does not have a right to enter the UK, and can still be turned away when they arrive.

Immigration law is the system of rules by which each country decides who is able to live in that country and under what conditions.

Nationality defines the country of which you are a citizen, and which usually issues you with a passport.

Naturalisation is the process of applying for British nationality. You can apply on the basis of residence in the UK, marriage to a British partner, or Crown service. The Home Office has discretion on whether to grant it or not.

Patriality is another word for 'right of abode'. It was first used in the Immigration Act 1971, but was replaced by the term 'right of abode' in the British Nationality Act 1981.

Public funds rule Before people to whom this applies get entry clearance, they have to show that they, or the sponsoring relatives, can support them without needing to apply for 'public funds'. For the purposes of the immigration rules, these mean Income Support, Family Credit, Housing Benefit, Council Tax Benefit, Attendance Allowance, Invalid Care Allowance, Severe Disablement Allowance, Disability Living Allowance, and the means-tested element of Jobseeker's Allowance; and housing for homeless people. See Chapters 7 and 8 for details of the people to whom this applies, and those who are exempt.

Reciprocal agreements These are treaties with certain countries on Social Security matters. With some of them your benefits (with or without annual increases, depending on the country) can be paid when you are abroad. Others only allow contributions to be added together ('aggregated'). There are leaflets available on each country from the DSS Pensions and Overseas Benefits Directorate (see pp 114–115).

Registration This can mean different things in British immigration and nationality law. For the purposes of this book, the important meanings are:

- *A process of applying for British nationality.* The word is now used for any child applying for British nationality, and for a person who holds any other kind of British nationality applying to become a British citizen.
- *Registering with the police.* People who are not Commonwealth or EEA citizens, who are over 16 and who have been allowed to remain in the UK for more than six months but are not settled may have to register with the police. This means going to the local police station, or the Aliens Registration Office in London, with the various documents required, and paying a fee to register.

Right of abode means being free of immigration control and able to enter the UK freely at any time, no matter how long after an absence. All British citizens have the right of abode, and so do some other Commonwealth citizens. These are people who were born before 1 January 1983 and had a parent born in the UK, and Commonwealth-citizen women married before 1 January 1983 to men who were born, registered or naturalised in the UK, or who were Commonwealth citizens with at least one parent born in the UK.

Settled This means someone who is legally in the UK, without any conditions (such as a time limit or restrictions on working while in the UK). Other terms used for this are 'permanent stay' and 'indefinite leave'. Most, but not all, settled people have a stamp in their passports saying that they have 'indefinite leave to remain in the UK'.

Stateless person Someone who is not a citizen of any country. In some cases, they will be travelling on documents issued by one particular country (such as British certificates of identity) but without having rights within that country.

Visa A form of entry clearance required for visa nationals (see below) coming to the UK.

Visa nationals People who always need to get entry clearance in advance of travelling to the UK, for whatever purpose, unless they are returning residents or are returning within a period of earlier leave granted for more than six months. A list of countries whose citizens are visa nationals is given in the *Immigration Law and Nationality Handbook*.

APPENDIX 2
Categories of countries for immigration and Social Security purposes

Commonwealth countries

Antigua and Barbuda	Australia
Bahamas	Bangladesh
Barbados	Belize
Botswana	Cameroon
Canada	Cyprus
Dominica	Gambia
Ghana	Grenada
Guyana	India
Jamaica	Kenya
Kiribati	Lesotho
Malawi	Malaysia
Malta	Mauritius
Mozambique	Namibia
Nauru	Nevis
New Zealand	Nigeria
Pakistan	Papua New Guinea
St Kitts	St Lucia

St Vincent and the Grenadines   Seychelles

Sierra Leone   Singapore

Solomon Islands   South Africa

Sri Lanka   Swaziland

Tanzania   Tonga

Trinidad and Tobago   Tuvalu

Uganda   Vanuatu

Western Samoa   Zambia

Zimbabwe

European Economic Area states

The European Economic Area consists of the 15 member states of the European Union:

Austria   Belgium

Denmark   Germany

Finland   France

Greece   Ireland

Italy   Luxembourg

The Netherlands   Portugal

Spain   Sweden

UK (including Gibraltar)

and three additional countries: Iceland, Liechtenstein and Norway

Countries from which entrants require a visa

Countries whose citizens are visa nationals in September 1996:

Afghanistan   Albania

Algeria   Angola

Armenia   Azerbaijan

Bahrain	Bangladesh
Belarus	Benin
Bhutan	Bosnia-Herzegovina
Bulgaria	Burkina Faso
Burma	Burundi
Cambodia	Cameroon
Cape Verde	Central African Republic
Chad	China
Comoros	Congo
Cuba	Djibouti
Dominican Republic	Egypt
Equatorial Guinea	Eritrea
Ethiopia	Fiji
Gabon	Gambia
Georgia	Ghana
Guinea	Guinea-Bissau
Guyana	Haiti
India	Indonesia
Iran	Iraq
Ivory Coast	Jordan
Kazakhstan	Kirgizstan
Korea (North)	Kuwait
Laos	Lebanon
Liberia	Libya
Macedonia	Madagascar
the Maldives	Mali

Mauretania	Mauritius
Moldova	Mongolia
Montenegro	Morocco
Mozambique	Nepal
Niger	Nigeria
Oman	Pakistan
Papua New Guinea	Peru
Philippines	Qatar
Romania	Russia
Rwanda	Sao Tome and Principe
Saudi Arabia	Senegal
Serbia	Sierra Leone
Somalia	Sri Lanka
Sudan	Surinam
Syria	Taiwan
Tajikistan	Thailand
Togo	Tunisia
Turkey	Turkmenistan
Uganda	United Arab Emirates
Uzbekistan	Vietnam
Yemen	Zaire
Zambia	

Countries with which there is a reciprocal Social Security agreement

Australia	Barbados
Bermuda	Canada

Cyprus	Israel
Jamaica	Malta
Mauritius	New Zealand
Philippines	Switzerland
Turkey	USA

The agreement with the former Yugoslavia is being honoured by remaining regions of the Federal Republic of Yugoslavia and by the states of Croatia, Slovenia and Bosnia-Herzegovina.

APPENDIX 3
Ethnic minority older people in Britain

Ethnic origin	Females ages 60 and over	Males aged 60 and over
White	6,659,513	4,800,009
Black: Caribbean	24,139	30,169
Black: African	2,192	3,490
Black: other	1,856	1,840
Indian	27,741	29,655
Pakistani	6,644	10,924
Bangladeshi	1,215	4,083
Chinese	4,787	4,117
Other: Asian	4,414	3,633
Other: other	7,450	7,116
Total (ethnic minorities)	80,438	95,027
Ireland	141,717	111,751
Total (ethnic minorities and white population):		
Excluding Ireland	6,739,951	4,895,036
Including Ireland	6,884,668	5,006,787

Source: Age and Race: *Double discrimination*, Overview section, p 3

The 1991 Census was the first to collect specific information on the UK's ethnic minority population. It defined ten different classifications of ethnicity. But its definitions do not include 'invisible minorities' such as Polish, Jewish and Cypriot people, so accurate figures for these groups are not recorded.

By far the largest 'immigrant' group is the Irish population, now numbering 211,000 people over pensionable age. They were not counted in the 1991 Census as part of the ethnic minority population (and so do not appear in the Table of this Appendix), but share many of the same problems such as prejudice, low incomes and cultural isolation.

Black Caribbeans, Chinese, Indians and Other Asians tend to be oldest; Black other, Other others, Bangladeshi and Pakistanis are the youngest. Black Caribbeans have the largest number of people of pensionable age, with 5.65 per cent aged 65 and over (10.9 per cent aged 60 and over), compared to only 1.2 per cent for the Bangladeshi population (3.3 per cent aged 60 or over.)

There is a 'middle-aged bulge' which means that the number of people of pensionable age will grow rapidly in the next 20–30 years. Among all ethnic groups there are currently 15.18 per cent of people aged between 45 and 64. Looking further ahead, the 25–44 age group is 32.49 per cent. This represents a ten-fold increase in numbers in 30–40 years' time.

Source: *Age and Race: Double discrimination*, Overview

APPENDIX 4
Useful publications

Age and Race; Double Discrimination; Life in Britain Today for Ethnic Minority Elders, CRE and Age Concern England (pack including a series of short papers), March 1995

Barriers to Benefits; Black Claimants and Social Security, NACAB, 1991, £5

Bridging the Language Barrier: A guide to communicating with deaf customers and provision of interpreting services, BA Publishing Services Ltd for BA Customer Services Branch, Room 2525, Quarry House, Leeds

Daily Telegraph Guide to Living Abroad, 1995, Kogan Page, London, £8.99

Guide to Living in Spain, Blackstone Franks, 1994, £6.99

Immigration and Nationality Law Handbook, Sue Shutter, JCWI (see p 118 for address), £12.99, new edition 1997

Migration and Social Security Handbook, 1997, published by Child Poverty Action Group, 1–5 Bath Street, London EC1V 9PY, £10.95

National Welfare Benefits Handbook, 1996/7, published by Child Poverty Action Group, £8.95

The Provision of Social Security Benefits to Minority Ethnic Communities, 1994, Social Policy Research 59, Joseph Rowntree Foundation, York

A Right to Family Life: CAB clients' experience of immigration and asylum, National Association of Citizens Advice Bureaux, 113–123 Pentonville Road, London N1 9LZ, March 1996

Where to Get Advice, Refugee Advisers Support Unit, The Refugee Council (see p 118 for address)

Your Rights: A guide to money benefits for older people, Sally West (see p 121)

Your Social Security rights when moving within the European Union: A practical guide, 1995, available from Social Security for Migrant Workers, DGV, European Commission, 200 rue de la Loi, Brussels, Belgium

APPENDIX 5
Relevant DSS leaflets

Current edition	Agency	Ref No	Publication Title
1995	BA	AACSS	*Attendance Allowance Charter Standard Statement* (also available in Chinese, Punjabi, Urdu)
Apr 1995	BA	BAL1	*Tell us about it* (also available in Arabic, Bengali, Chinese, Greek, Gujarati, Hindi, Punjabi, Somali, Turkish, Urdu and Vietnamese)
Jul 1994	BA	BAL4	*Providing evidence of your identity* (also available in Arabic, Bengali, Chinese, Greek, Gujarati, Hindi, Punjabi, Somali, Turkish, Urdu and Vietnamese)
Apr 1995	BA	CTB2	*Help with the Council Tax* (also available in Arabic, Bengali, Chinese, Greek, Gujarati, Hindi, Punjabi, Somali, Turkish, Urdu and Vietnamese)
Dec 1993	BA	CUST1	*Benefits Agency Customer Charter* (also available in Arabic, Bengali, Chinese, Greek, Gujarati, Hindi, Punjabi, Somali, Turkish, Urdu and Vietnamese)
1995	BA	DLACSS	*Disability Living Allowance Charter Standard Statement* (also available in Chinese, Punjabi, Urdu)

Apr 1996	BA	DS 702	*Attendance Allowance* (also available in Arabic, Bengali, Chinese, Greek, Gujarati, Hindi, Punjabi, Turkish, Urdu and Vietnamese)
Apr 1996	BA	DS 704	*Disability Living Allowance – You could benefit* (also available in Bengali, Chinese, Greek, Gujarati, Hindi, Punjabi, Turkish, Urdu and Vietnamese)
	BA	EP1/P	*If you want an interpreter please ask* (**poster** – also available in Bengali, Chinese, Gujarati, Hindi, Punjabi, Somali, Turkish and Vietnamese)
	BA	EP2/P	*Which Benefit?* (**poster** – also available in Bengali, Chinese, Gujarati, Hindi, Punjabi, Somali, Turkish and Vietnamese)
Jan 1996	BA	FB 22	*Which Benefit?* (available in Arabic, Bengali, Chinese, Greek, Gujarati, Hindi, Punjabi, Somali, Turkish and Vietnamese)
	BA	GEN 21/P	*Do you know your benefit rights?* (**poster** in Chinese)
	BA	GEN 22/P	*Do you know your benefit rights?* (**poster** in Urdu)
	BA	GEN 23/P	*Do you know your benefit rights?* (**poster** in Bengali)
	BA	GEN 24/P	*Do you know your benefit rights?* (**poster** in Hindi)
	BA	GEN 25/P	*Do you know your benefit rights?* (**poster** in Punjabi)
	BA	GEN 26/P	*Do you know your benefit rights?* (**poster** in Gujarati)

	BA	GEN 27/P	*Do you know your benefit rights?* (**poster** in Turkish)
	BA	GEN 28/P	*Do you know your benefit rights?* (poster in Vietnamese)
	BA	GEN 29/P	*Do you know your benefit rights?* (**poster** in Somali)
	BA	GEN 30/P	*Do you know your benefit rights?* (**poster** in Arabic)
	BA	GEN 31/P	*Help and advice on Social Security benefits* (**poster** – also available in Arabic, Bengali, Chinese, Greek, Gujarati, Hindi, Punjabi, Somali, Turkish, Urdu and Vietnamese)
	BA	GEN 32/P	*Do you know your benefit rights?* (**poster** in Greek)
	DoH	HC 10*	*Help with health costs* (**poster** – also available in Bengali, Chinese, Gujarati, Hindi, Punjabi and Urdu)
Feb 1995	BA	IB 201	(**audio**) *Incapacity Benefit – a guide for people getting Sickness Benefit, Invalidity Benefit, Severe Disablement Allowance, disability premium paid with Income Support, Housing Benefit or Council Tax Benefit* (also available in Gujarati, Hindi, Sylheti and Urdu)
Apr 1993	BA	LBF 1	*Let's be fair* (also available in Arabic, Bengali, Chinese, Greek, Gujarati, Hindi, Punjabi, Somali, Turkish, Urdu and Vietnamese)
Apr 1993	BA	LBF 1/P	*Let's be fair* (**poster** – also available in Arabic, Bengali, Chinese, Greek, Gujarati, Hindi, Punjabi, Somali, Turkish, Urdu and Vietnamese)

Apr 1996	BA	NP45	*A Guide to Widows' Benefits*
Apr 1996	BA	NP46	*A Guide to Retirement Pensions*
Apr 1995	BA	RR 1	*Housing Benefit – help with your rent* (also available in Arabic, Bengali, Chinese, Greek, Gujarati, Hindi, Punjabi, Somali, Turkish, Urdu and Vietnamese)
Sep 1994	BA	SA 4	*Social Security agreement between the United Kingdom and Jersey and Guernsey*
Sep 1994	BA	SA 5	*Social Security agreement between the United Kingdom and Australia*
Sep 1994	BA	SA 6	*Social Security agreement between the United Kingdom and Switzerland*
Sep 1994	BA	SA 8	*Social Security agreement between the United Kingdom and New Zealand*
Sep 1994	BA	SA 11	*Social Security agreement between the United Kingdom and Malta*
Sep 1994	BA	SA 12	*Social Security agreement between the United Kingdom and Cyprus*
Sep 1994	BA	SA 14	*Social Security agreement between the United Kingdom and Israel*
Sep 1994	BA	SA 17	*Social Security agreement between the United Kingdom and Yugoslavia*
Sep 1994	BA	SA 20	*Social Security agreement between the United Kingdom and Canada*
Sep 1994	BA	SA 22	*Social Security agreement between the United Kingdom and Turkey*
Sep 1994	BA	SA 23	*Social Security agreement between the United Kingdom and Bermuda*

Sep 1994	BA	SA 27	*Social Security agreement between the United Kingdom and Jamaica*
Sep 1994	BA	SA 29	*Your Social Security insurance benefits and health care rights in the European Community, and in Iceland, Liechtenstein and Norway*
Sep 1994	BA	SA 33	*Social Security agreement between the United Kingdom and the United States of America*
1 Sep 1994	BA	SA 38	*Social Security agreement between the United Kingdom and Mauritius*
Sep 1994	BA	SA 42	*Social Security agreement between the United Kingdom and the Philippines*
Sep 1994	BA	SA 43	*Social Security agreement between the United Kingdom and Barbados*
May 1996	BA	SFL 2	*How the Social Fund can help you* (also available in Arabic, Bengali, Chinese, Greek, Gujarati, Hindi, Punjabi, Somali, Turkish, Urdu and Vietnamese)
Dec 1995		TA 3	(**audio**) *Pensions and retirement* (also available in Chinese, Gujarati, Hindi, Polish, Punjabi, Somali, Sylheti, Turkish, Urdu and Vietnamese)
Dec 1995		TA 4	(**audio**) *Sick or disabled?* (also available in Chinese, Gujarati, Hindi, Polish, Punjabi, Somali, Sylheti, Turkish, Urdu and Vietnamese)
Sep 1995	WPA	WPA 1	*Notes about war pensions and allowances*

Sep 1995	WPA	WPA 3	*Notes for people getting a war pension* (overseas)
Sep 1995	WPA	WPA 5	*Notes for people not getting a war pension* (overseas)
Sep 1995	WPA	WPA 6	*Notes for war pensioners and war widows going abroad*
Sep 1995	WPA	WPA 7	*Notes about ex–Far East and Korean prisoners of war*

APPENDIX 6
Useful addresses

Age Concern Spain (Baleares), c/o Banco de Credito Balear, Plaza Major 28-Buzon 22, 07650 Santanyi, Mallorca, Spain. Tel: +34 71 16 34 62

Aliens Registration Office, 10 Lamb's Conduit Street, London WC1X 3MX. Tel: 0171-725 2451

The police station where some people from abroad living in London may be required to register their personal details.

Benefits Agency, Pensions and Overseas Benefits Directorate, Tyneview Park, Benton, Whitley Road, Newcastle upon Tyne NE98 1BA. Tel: 0191-218 7777

Deals with claims for retirement pensions, and for National Insurance benefits where someone has had a period of time in another country, or is asking for them to be paid abroad.

British Red Cross Society, Family Reunion Section, 9 Grosvenor Crescent, London SW1X 7EJ

Provides advice on refugee family reunion procedures and resettlement from a third country (that is, from another country that is not your own country). Co-ordinates applications for travel assistance for refugee family reunion.

Commission for Racial Equality, Elliot House, 10–12 Allington Street, London SW1E 5EH. Tel: 0171-828 7022

Advises a variety of agencies on how to avoid discrimination. Also publishes guidance and codes of practice to help organisations achieve equality of opportunity.

Foreign and Commonwealth Office, Consular Division, Clive House, Petty France, London SW1H 9HD. Tel: 0171-270 4123

Runs embassies and consulates abroad, and may be able to provide information about benefits elsewhere (or tell you where to enquire).

Home Office Immigration and Nationality Directorate, Lunar House, Wellesley Road, Croydon, CR9 2BY. Main tel: 0181-686 0688; fax: 0181-760 1181. Public enquiry office open 9 am to 4 pm, Monday to Friday.

Deals with all immigration and nationality applications in the UK. Once you have a Home Office reference number, you will be given a specific phone number to contact with any queries. The Application Forms Unit (tel: 0181-760 2233) in that office sends out the forms for applications to appeal against immigration decisions.

Immigration Advisory Service (head office), County House, 190 Great Dover Street, London SE1 4YB. 24-hour helpline: 0181-814 1559; ordinary tel: 0171-357 6917; fax: 0171-378 0665

Also has offices around the country, including Heathrow and Gatwick. Government-supported agency giving advice and guidance on immigration problems, concentrating on representation at immigration appeals.

International Social Service of Great Britain, Cranmer House, 39 Brixton Road, London SW9 6DD. Tel: 0171-735 8941; fax: 0171-582 0696

Runs system of repatriation grants for Government.

Joint Council for the Welfare of Immigrants, 115 Old Street, London EC1V 9JR. Tel: 0171-251 8706 (advice), 0171-251 8708 (admin); fax: 0171-251 8707

Can provide specialist advice for anyone having problems with immigration authorities; publishes a Handbook and other literature. But very overburdened, so try to take simpler enquiries elsewhere.

Refugee Arrivals Project, Room 2005, 2nd Floor, Queens Building, Heathrow Airport, TW6 1DL. Tel: 0181-739 5740; fax: 0181-739 1528

Can advise and help asylum seekers to find accommodation and financial support, and seek release of those initially detained.

Refugee Council, 3 Bondway, London SW8 1SJ. Tel: 0171-582 6922; fax: 0171-582 9927

Provides a national focal point for voluntary agencies working with refugees, with direct assistance and advice on benefits to those seeking asylum in the UK. Can also give information on refugee community organisations and how to contact them. Runs Agnew House, a home for elderly refugees.

Refugee Legal Centre, Sussex House, 39–45 Bermondsey Street, London SE1 3XP. Tel: 0171-827 9090

Advice and free representation at all stages of an application for asylum in the UK.

Royal British Legion, 48 Pall Mall, London SW1Y 5JY. Tel: 0171-973 7200

Britain's premier ex-service organisation for the welfare of ex-service-men, women and their dependants. Provides financial assistance, and residential and convalescent homes. Also provides social focus for ex-service community in branches and clubs throughout England, Wales and all Ireland.

Soldiers', Sailors' & Airmen's Families Association (SSAFA), 19 Queen Elizabeth Street, London SE1 2LP. Tel: 0171-403 8783

A national charity helping serving and ex-servicemen and women and families in need.

Standing Conference of Ethnic Minority Senior Citizens (SCEMSC), 5 Westminster Bridge Road, London SE1 7XW. Tel: 0171-928 0095

Provides support, training and development skills to community and day centres, working with older people from ethnic minority groups.

War Pensions Agency, Norcross, Blackpool FY5 3WP. Helpline: 01253 858858

Runs the system of war pensions for the DSS and helps war veterans with other problems.

About Age Concern

Ethnic Elders' Benefits Handbook is one of a wide range of publications produced by Age Concern England, the National Council on Ageing. Age Concern England is actively engaged in training, information provision, fundraising and campaigning for retired people and those who work with them, and also in the provision of products and services such as insurance for older people.

A network of over 1,400 local Age Concern groups, with the support of around 250,000 volunteers, aims to improve the quality of life for older people and develop services appropriate to local needs and resources. These include advice and information, day care, visiting services, transport schemes, clubs, and specialist facilities for older people who are physically and mentally frail.

Age Concern England is a registered charity dependent on public support for the continuation and development of its work.

Age Concern England
1268 London Road
London SW16 4ER
Tel: 0181-679 8000

Age Concern Scotland
113 Rose Street
Edinburgh EH2 3DT
Tel: 0131-220 3345

Age Concern Cymru
4th Floor
1 Cathedral Road
Cardiff CF1 9SD
Tel: 01222 371566

Age Concern Northern Ireland
6 Lower Crescent
Belfast BT7 1NR
Tel: 01232 245729

Publications from Age Concern Books

MONEY MATTERS

Your Rights: A guide to money benefits for older people
Sally West

A highly successful annual publication – now in its 25th edition – *Your Rights* guides readers through the maze of money benefits for older people and explains what you can claim and why. Specific sections are provided on: retirement pensions, housing and council tax benefits, benefits for disabled people, Income Support and the Social Fund, funeral payments, paying for fuel, insulation and repairs, paying for residential care and help with legal and health costs.

For further information, please ring 0181-679 8000.

Managing Other People's Money
Penny Letts
Foreword by the Master of The Court of Protection

This book is a step-by-step guide to the arrangements that need to be made to manage other people's money on either a temporary or a permanent basis. Invaluable for individuals who need to 'step in', this book also contains expert guidance for legal advisers and other advice workers.

£3.99   0–86242–090–3

PROFESSIONAL, POLICY & RESEARCH

The Community Care Handbook: The reformed system explained
Barbara Meredith

Written by one of the country's leading experts, the second edition of this hugely successful handbook provides a comprehensive overview of the first two years of implementation of the community care reforms and examines how the system has evolved. Containing extensive background information on the origins of the new system, this edition describes some of the experiences of those working in the field.

£13.99   0–86242–171–3

Caring for Ethnic Minority Elders: A guide

Yasmin Alibhai-Brown

A practical guide to the delivery of care to older people from ethnic minority groups, this book highlights the impact of varying cultural traditions and stresses their significance in the design of individual care packages.

£14.99   0-86242–188–8   Available January 1988

If you would like to order any of these titles, please write to the address below, enclosing a cheque or money order for the appropriate amount made payable to Age Concern England. Credit card orders may be made on 0181-679 8000.

Mail Order Unit
Age Concern England
1268 London Road
London SW16 4ER

Factsheets from Age Concern

Covering many areas of concern to older people, Age Concern's factsheets are comprehensive and totally up to date. There are more than 30 factsheets and each one provides straightforward information and impartial advice in a simple and easy-to-use format. Among these, the following may be of interest to readers of this book:

1 Help with heating

5 Dental care in retirement

10 Local authority charging procedures for residential and nursing home care

11 Preserved rights to Income Support for residential and nursing homes

16 Income related benefits: income and capital

17 Housing Benefit and Council Tax Benefit

18 A brief guide to money benefits

21 The Council Tax and older people

25 Income Support and the Social Fund

32 Disability and ageing: your rights to social services

34 Attendance Allowance and Disability Living Allowance

Single copies are available free on receipt of a 9" × 12" sae.

Age Concern offers a factsheet subscription service which presents all the factsheets in a folder, together with regular updates throughout the year. The first year's subscription currently costs £40; an annual renewal thereafter is £20.

For a free list of all factsheets, or to order copies, send a large sae to:

Information Services Division
Age Concern England
1268 London Road
London SW16 4ER

Index

accommodation: and immigration
26
Adjudication Officers 43, 44
Adult Dependency Allowance 54
advice, getting 3–4
age, proving 53–54
Age Concern 120
  publications 3, 4, 121–123
aggregation rule 49, 53, 97
'aliens' 6, 9, 13, 97
allowances *see* benefits and
  allowances
Antigua and Barbuda 8
appeals:
  immigration 33–36
  Social Security 43–45
armed forces 14
  see also War Pensions
Asian population 107, 108
Asylum and Immigration Acts 26,
31
asylum seekers 22, 31–32
  appeals system 33, 36
  and benefits 33, 74–77, 78–79,
  84
Attendance Allowance 39, 41, 50,
67

Bangladeshi population 2, 107, 108
BDTCs *see* British Dependent

Territories citizens
Belize 8
benefits and allowances:
  advice on 3, 4
  and aggregation rule 49, 53, 97
  appeals 43–45
  claiming 1–2, 41–43, 47–48
  contributory and non-
  contributory 39, 51
  'exporting' 49–50
  means-tested 39, 40
  and reciprocal agreements 48,
  53, 100, 105–106
  requesting reviews of 43
Benefits Agency 40
  and equal opportunities 40–41
  and Home Office 47–48
  and language difficulties 45–46
British citizens 7, 17, 98
  applying to be 14–16
  born overseas 13–14
  by descent 14, 97
British Council workers 14
British Dependent Territories
  Citizens (BDTCs) 7, 8, 9, 12
British Empire 5
British Nationality Acts 6, 7–8, 12
British nationals 6, 10, 11, 14, 98
  with East African connection 11
  from Hong Kong 12–13

and registration 15–16
who are not British citizens 11
British Nationals (Overseas) 7, 12, 98
British Overseas citizens 7, 8, 9, 11, 38, 98
British Protected Persons 6, 7, 8, 9, 98
British subjects 6–7, 8, 9, 10, 98
'without citizenship' 6, 7–8, 9

Caribbean population 8, 107, 108
certificates of entitlement 10, 17
certificates of identity 8, 12, 98
certificates of patriality 17
see also 'patriality'
Channel Islands 18, 20, 40, 70, 75
Child Poverty Action Group 3, 4
Chinese population 2, 4, 107, 108
from Hong Kong 12
Citizen of the United Kingdom and Colonies (CUKC) 6–7
claims, making:
for benefits 1–2, 41–43, 47–48
for pensions 57
Common Travel Area (CTA) 18, 70, 75
Commonwealth, the 5, 102–103
citizens 6, 7, 17, 18, 98–99
Commonwealth Immigrants Acts 11, 12
community care:
grants 83, 84
see also residential and nursing homes
'conditions of entry' 99
Contributions Agency 40
Council Tax Benefit 39, 69, 81–82
Counsel and Care 92, 93
Crisis Loans 78, 84
CTA *see* Common Travel Area

CUKC *see* Citizen of the United Kingdom and Colonies
Cypriot population 70, 108

dental care 89
Department of Social Security 40
leaflets 111–116
see also Benefits Agency
'dependency' 25
deportation 29, 30
diplomats 14
disability benefits 40, 41
see also Attendance Allowance;
Disability Living Allowance;
Invalid Care Allowance; Severe Disablement Allowance; War Pensions
Disability Living Allowance 41, 50, 66–67
doctors *see* general practitioners
'domicile' 37, 55, 99
domiciliary help 92
DSS *see* Department of Social Security

East African population 7, 11
EEA *see* European Economic Area employment
'entry clearance' 21, 99
EU *see* European Union
European Economic Area (EEA) 13, 18, 19, 58, 70, 103
and benefits 49–50
in EU countries 19
and 'exporting' of benefits 49–50
'family permit' 20
and health costs 89–90
and immigration of parents and grandparents 24
and National Insurance contributions 51–53

European Economic Community 13

European Union (EU) 13, 19–20, 103

'exceptional leave to remain' 32–33

'exporting' benefits 49–50

eye tests 89

Falkland Islands 5, 7

Family Credit 39

family permits, EEA 20

funeral costs 84–86

general practitioners, registering with 87

Gibraltar 5

glasses 89

GPs *see* general practitioners

Graduated Pension 59

grandparents:
  and conferring of British citizenship 14
  immigration of 24–25

'habitual residence' 20, 38, 70–73

health care 87
  abroad 89–90
  compulsory costs of 89
  from general practitioners 87
  hospital charges 87–89, 90
  private (for 'medical visitors') 90–91

help, getting 3–4

Home Responsibility Protection 54

homes, care *see* residential and nursing homes

Hong Kong, people from 7, 8, 12–13

hospitals:
  charges 87–89, 90
  travel costs 89

Housing Benefit 39, 41, 69, 81–82

Iceland 19

'illegal entrants' 24, 29–30, 77–78, 84
  and benefits 47–48, 77–78, 84

immigration 3, 5, 17–18
  appeals 23, 33–36
  controls/'leave to enter' 20–21, 22–23
  of dependent relatives 20, 21, 23–24, 25
  of EU citizens 19–20
  of Irish nationals 20
  of parents and grandparents 24–25
  records 48
  of retired people 21–22
  of returning residents 37–38
  sponsored 23, 24, 26, 64, 73–74
  see also asylum seekers; illegal entrants; 'overstayers'; refugee status; visitors

Immigration Appeals Tribunal 33, 35, 36

Incapacity Benefit 39, 41, 60–62
  'exporting' 49–50

Income Support 39, 40, 69
  for asylum seekers 74–77
  claiming 47–48, 79–80
  and 'habitual residence' rule 20, 68, 70–73
  and illegal entrants 47–48, 77
  and 'persons from abroad' 70, 77–78
  and sponsored immigrants 73–74

India:
  Pension Liaison Officers 42, 48
  voucher scheme 11

Indian population 6, 23, 107, 108

interpreting services 45–46, 93

Invalid Care Allowance 39, 67–68
Ireland, Republic of/Irish
   immigrants 18, 20, 70, 75, 107,
   108
Isle of Man 18, 20, 40, 75

JCWI 3
Jewish population 108
Joint Council for the Welfare of
   Immigrants (JCWI) 3

Kenyans 11

language:
   difficulties 29, 45–46, 93
   requirements for naturalisation
   14, 15
'leave to enter' 20–21, 22–23
Liechtenstein 19
loans:
   budgeting 83
   crisis 78, 84

Maltese nationals 70
marriage:
   and immigration 19, 20, 21, 24
   and legitimation of children 10
   and naturalisation 15
   validity of 55–57
married women:
   and naturalisation 15
   pensions for 54–55
   and right of abode 7, 8
   see also widows
medical insurance 89
'medical visitors' 23, 90–91
Montserrat, people from 70
Muslim Family Laws Ordinance 57

names, confusion over 47
National Health Service (NHS):
   charges 39, 89

general practitioners 87
hospital charges 87–89
prescriptions 89
National Insurance contributions
   39, 40, 45, 51–52
   and confusion over names 47
nationality 5, 99
nationality law 3, 5
naturalisation 14–15, 99
Nigeria 6, 55
Northern Ireland 40, 81
Norway 19
nursing homes *see* residential and
   nursing homes

Ouseley, Herman 92
'overstayers' 29, 30
   and benefits 47–48, 77–78, 84

Pakistani population 2, 6, 57, 107,
   108
parents:
   and children's citizenship 13–14
   dependent 19, 24–25
passports 5, 8, 10, 17, 18, 23, 53
'patriality' 7, 99
pensioners:
   in European Union 19–20
   see also pensions; retired people
pensions:
   basic State *see* retirement
   pensions
   SERPs 59
   war 41, 94–95
   widows' 39, 41, 49–50, 59–60
Pensions and Overseas Benefits
   Directorate (POD) 40, 42, 43, 48
'persons from abroad' 70, 74,
   77–78
POD *see* Pensions and Overseas
   Benefits Directorate

police, registering with the 100
Polish population 108
prescriptions 89
  abroad 90
'presence' 65
'public funds' rules 11, 20, 26, 77,
  99–100

'quota voucher' scheme 11, 16

Racial Equality Council (REC) 4
reciprocal Social Security
  agreements 48, 53, 100, 105–106
Refugee Council 3
refugee status 31, 32
registration 15–16, 100
relatives, immigration of 19, 20,
  23–24, 25
repatriation 30
'residence' 64
  habitual 20, 38, 70–73
  ordinary 37–38, 64–65
residence permits, applying for 20
residential and nursing homes:
  acceptable services in 92–93
  paying for 91–92
retired people:
  immigration of 19–20, 21–22
  see also retirement pensions
retirement pensions 39
  claiming 41, 57
  and going abroad 49–50, 57–58
  increases in 58
  for people over 80 59
  qualifying for 51–53
  and reciprocal agreements 48,
  53, 58
right of abode 6, 8, 10, 17, 18, 100

St Kitts-Nevis 8
SERPS 59

'settlement'/'settled status' 14, 37,
  100–101
  of dependent relatives 23–24
Severe Disablement Allowance 41,
  63–65
  'exporting' 49–50
Social Fund 69, 78, 83
Social Security 39–41
  see also benefits and allowances;
  Benefits Agency
Social Security Appeal Tribunal
  (SSAT) 43
social services *see* community care
solicitors 3
spectacles 89
sponsorship:
  of immigrants 23, 24, 26, 47,
  64, 73–74
  of visitors 28
SSAT *see* Social Security Appeal
  Tribunal 43
stateless person 8, 21, 101

Turkey/Turkish nationals 19, 70

Ugandans 11
Urgent Cases Payments 73, 74, 77

visa nationals 20, 21, 101, 103–105
visas 18, 101
visitors, UK 27–28, 33
vouchers *see* 'quota voucher' scheme

War Pensions 41, 94–95
Welfare Rights Officers 4
widows:
  benefits and pensions for 39, 41,
  49–50, 59–60
  immigration of 24, 25
work *see* employment
'working life' 52